MW00784489

WICCA STARTER KIT

2 Manuscripts:

Wicca for Beginner

Wiccan Spells

Dora McGregor

© Copyright 2019 Dora McGregor

All rights reserved

Wicca Starter Kit

© Copyright 2019 Dora McGregor All rights reserved.

Written by Dora McGregor

First Edition

Copyrights Notice

No part of this book may be reproduced in any form or by any electronic or mechanical means, including information storage and retrieval systems, without written permission from the author.

Recording of this publication is strictly prohibited and any storage of this document is not allowed unless with written permission from the publisher.

All rights reserved. Respective authors all copyrights not held by the publisher.

Pictures inside this book are of the respective ers, granted to the Author in a Royalty-Free license.

All trademarks, service marks, product names, and the characteristics of any names mentioned in this book are considered the property of their respective ers and are used only for reference. No endorsement is implied when we use one of these terms.

Limited Liability

Please note that the content of this book is based on personal experience and various information sources, and it is only for personal use.

Please note the information contained within this document is for educational and entertainment purposes only and no warranties of any kind are declared or implied.

Readers acknowledge that the author is not engaging in the rendering of legal, financial, or professional advice. Please consult a licensed professional before attempting any techniques outlined in this book.

Nothing in this book is intended to replace common sense or legal accounting, or professional advice and is meant only to inform.

Your particular circumstances may not be suited to the example illustrated in this book; in fact, they likely will not be.

You should use the information in this book at your risk. The reader is responsible for his or her actions.

The information provided herein is stated to be truthful and consistent, in that any liability, in terms of inattention or otherwise, by any usage or abuse of any policies, processes, or directions contained within is the solitary and utter responsibility of the recipient reader.

By reading this book, the reader agrees that under no circumstances is the author responsible for any losses, direct or indirect, which are incurred as a result of the use of the information contained within this document, including, but not limited to, errors, omissions, or inaccuracies.

YOUR FREE GIFT!!

Thank you for adding this book to your Wiccan Library! To learn more, why not join Dora's Wiccan Community and **get an exclusive free spells book?**

Little Grimoire of Wicca Spells is a great starting point for anyone looking to try their hand to practicing magic and **include 10 beginner-friendly spells** can help you to create a positive atmosphere within your home, protect yourself from negativity, and attract love, health, and prosperity.

Little Grimoire of Wicca Spells **is now available to read on your laptop, phone, tablet, Kindle, Kobo or Nook device.**

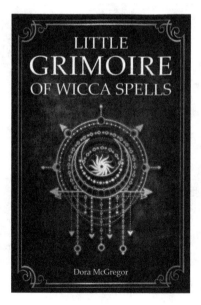

To download for free simply visit the following link:

www.wiccantribe.com/freebook

Download WICCA STARTER KIT in Audio Book version for FREE!!

Did you know that all of Dora's books are available in audiobook format? Best of all, you can get 2 audiobooks **completely FREE as part of a 30-day trial with Audible.**

Audible members receive free audiobooks every month, as well as exclusive discounts. It's a great way to experiment and see if audiobook learning works for you.

If you're not satisfied, you can cancel anytime within the trial period. You won't be charged, and you can still keep your books!

To download simply visit the following link:

www.wiccantribe.com/wiccastarter

page intentionally left blank

WICCA FOR BEGINNERS

Wiccan Traditions and Beliefs, Witchcraft Philosophy, Practical Magic, Candle, Crystals and Herbal Rituals

Dora McGregor

© Copyright 2019 Dora McGregor

All rights reserved

Wicca for Beginners

© Copyright 2019 Dora McGregor All rights reserved.

Written by Dora McGregor

First Edition

Copyrights Notice

No part of this book may be reproduced in any form or by any electronic or mechanical means, including information storage and retrieval systems, without written permission from the author.

Recording of this publication is strictly prohibited and any storage of this document is not allowed unless with written permission from the publisher.

All rights reserved. Respective authors all copyrights not held by the publisher.

Pictures inside this book are of the respective ers, granted to the Author in a Royalty-Free license.

All rights reserved. Respective authors all copyrights not held by the publisher.

All trademarks, service marks, product names, and the characteristics of any names mentioned in this book are considered the property of their respective ers and are used only for reference. No endorsement is implied when we use one of these terms.

Limited Liability

Please note that the content of this book is based on personal experience and various information sources, and it is only for personal use.

Please note the information contained within this document is for educational and entertainment purposes only and no warranties of any kind are declared or implied.

Readers acknowledge that the author is not engaging in the rendering of legal, financial, or professional advice. Please consult a licensed professional before attempting any techniques outlined in this book.

Nothing in this book is intended to replace common sense or legal accounting, or professional advice and is meant only to inform.

Your particular circumstances may not be suited to the example illustrated in this book; in fact, they likely will not be.

You should use the information in this book at your risk. The reader is responsible for his or her actions.

The information provided herein is stated to be truthful and consistent, in that any liability, in terms of inattention or otherwise, by any usage or abuse of any policies, processes, or directions contained within is the solitary and utter responsibility of the recipient reader.

By reading this book, the reader agrees that under no circumstances is the author responsible for any losses, direct or indirect, which are incurred as a result of the use of the information contained within this document, including, but not limited to, errors, omissions, or inaccuracies.

Table of Contents

Introduction

A Wiccan is someone who believes in the religion of Wicca who has knowledge of Pagans or follows their paths provided by Wicca. People who follow the Wiccan religion go by one saying which is very important: "Harm none, do what you will."

It states that if you are not harming anyone, then you are free to believe in whatever you would like and act as you please.

It does not force you to follow certain religious books and it does not include any supposed rules for you to follow. Wicca is all about teaching you how to allow yourself patience and self-care while being able to fully work on your spiritual and physical growth.

With Wicca, you can practice meditation and learn how to be self-aware while also being aware of what is around you. You can recognize what is unhealthy and make decisions to change.

Like Buddhism, Wicca helps you work solely on yourself and redefine your spiritual, mental, and physical being. Once you know your true self, you can develop further and will have the confidence to tackle whatever comes at you.

Chapter 1

The history of Wicca

Many of the traditions of Wicca come from more ancient Pagan belief systems and practices, however, the advent of Wicca and its founding philosophies originated in England and was introduced in the mid-1950s by a British civil servant by the name of Gerald Gardner.

A basic idea of Wicca is that it is considered what some might term Neo-Paganism, however, some distinct qualities and characteristics set it apart from the traditional denominations of the paganism practiced in more ancient cultures.

Before Gardner introduced Wicca to the public in 1954, the concepts of Wicca could be traced back to a woman named Margaret Murray who was a renewed folklorist, anthropologist and Egyptologist, who studied the traditions and cultures of a wide range of religious practices, combining a field study of these sects and describing in her words the concept of witchcraft.

Murray wrote a large set of books about medieval religious practices, specifically those centered on witch-cults in Europe.

Her works inspired readers to rekindle the pagan arts by creating their covens, structuring their worship around the descriptions from Murray's books. All of this was going on in the early 1920s in Great Britain and Europe and likely led to Gerald Gardner's more structured philosophy called Wicca.

Gardener's book entitled *Witchcraft Today* demonstrated the origin of the word Wicca and what it means to the craft. In his book, it is spelled with only one 'c', as in "wica", and it wasn't until the 1960's that the second 'c' was added. Gardner mentions that the word 'wica' is a Gaelic, or Scots-English word meaning "wise people". He had always had an interest in the occult and eventually became initiated into a coven of his in the late 1930s. Eventually, he formed his coven in the late '40s, buying land and establishing it as a center for the study of folklore. It became his occult headquarters and where he would bring to light the Wiccan way through his writing and practice.

A great connection existed between Gardner and the famed occultist Aleister Crowley. The two men met in the late 1940s and had much to discuss their personal beliefs and magic.

Gardner's work and writing out of his rituals of Wicca for publication were strongly influenced by Crowley's work, which had dated back to the earlier part of the century.

Gardner published his works, one of them is a novel entitled, *High Magic's Aid*, which became one of his first standard tomes to describe the practice of Wicca.

It was his *Book of Shadows*, however, that became the most highly regarded and sought after. Gardner's Book of Shadows was his collection of spells, rituals, and other information about the craft. To this day, it is one of the most central books for the practice of Wicca, or at least for learning from the original Wiccan, Gardner himself.

Fortunately, Wicca was then, and remains to be, an ever-evolving practice and does not adhere to a strict set of rules.

It happens to be a very flexible religion and offers that people follow a simple set of ideas and concepts and that there is freedom within those ideas to explore and form a deeper understanding.

Initiates of Gardner's coven were given the Book of Shadows to copy out and use and that was one of the ways they belonged to the coven, sharing the same spells and rituals to carry forward and practice. Gardner met Doreen Valiente in the early 1950s before Wicca had it coming out.

She contacted him after seeing an article in a magazine about covens, witches, their practices, and what that reality was like. Under Gardner's guidance, she was able to revise *The Book of Shadows* for Gardner to offer it as a popular book for others outside of the coven and also prominent Wiccan circles, similar to how Crowley had marketed his beliefs and findings.

Valiente became a Wiccan leader of her coven and was a prominent figure and scholar in the world of steadily growing Wiccans. The story of Wicca, when you look at it like that, seems like no more than a trifle in the annals of history, but when you look a little deeper, it had a profound impact on the world of magic.

Leading up to Gardner's exposure of his new religion, there were several ways that people were still looking to practice the ancient Pagan arts. Witchcraft was an incredibly taboo practice for centuries after the witch trials.

The study of the past by Margaret Murray helped people to find a new appreciation and understanding for the beauty of this magic and if it wasn't for her work, and that of other occult philosophers, Wicca might not have been born. To be honest, it has always existed in some form or fashion and it has carried many other names. The big umbrella term for it would be Pagan, and that word houses a whole cornucopia of possible sects and denominations, practices, and rituals. So then, it begs the question: what makes Wicca different?

Based on nature worship of the pagan religions, modern-day Wicca approaches connection to the divine through rituals and practices, festivals of the solstices, observances of deities, specifically a male and female god form, herbalism, a code of ethics and a belief in reincarnation and an afterlife. Some say that it is a modern-day interpretation of those pagan religions and traditions, which existed before Christianity.

It has its origins in Europe, but in today's world will also incorporate concepts from other religious practices like Shamanism and pre-Christian Egyptian religion. It has been noted that there are strong similarities to Druidism, as well, despite there being a lack of evidence about how the Druids truly worshipped.

A majority of Wiccans are duotheistic, meaning they worship a male god and a female goddess, or the Horned God and Mother Goddess, or Mother Earth. It is not always the case and even the early forms of Wicca, back in Gardner's day, were not strict. Most of the time, it was determined on a coven by coven basis, what deities would be worshiped by the group and how to perform certain rituals. Some other forms of Wiccan practice involve, and are not limited to, atheism, pantheism, and polytheism.

This opens the playing field to anyone wishing to establish a Wiccan practice, involving all of the other ethics and rituals into their work while getting the chance to determine how they want to worship.

The basics remain the same, but the deities or what gets worshipped changes. Apart from these components outlined in the earliest forms of Wicca, there is a devout appreciation for the Earth and all of her inhabitants which is why Wicca tends to be called a nature-based religion.

The use of herbs and plants in spell work and rituals is celebrated regularly, and also includes a devotion to the seasons of the Earth cycles and Moon cycles, bringing focus to all living rhythms.

The history of Wicca may feel recent; however, it comes from a long and green history of pagans, druids, witches, warlocks, and all of the individuals and covens along the way who had a sincere devotion to the presence of Earth magic and all of its gifts.

Giving attention to the origins of Wicca is an important beginning to your study and as you embrace the methods of how Wicca can be practiced, like those before you, you can build upon it to make it work for you the way that feels best. There are only guidelines and no strict rules. Wicca is meant to evolve with the individual, and whether you are practicing alone or in a group, the Wicca of the past will always be a part of the Wicca of the present. Your Wicca.

Wiccan Philosophy

Wicca can be described as a broad religion as it has the happiness of including a lot of different perspectives, realities, and beliefs.

There are, however, several major core beliefs that are practiced by a majority of Wiccans as a way to establish a grounding basis for understanding the magic you are working with when you are practicing.

These concepts are taken into account, no matter what coven you are in, or what deity you are worshipping. The concepts outlined in this chapter are the main platform, or foundation, of what Wicca is and how it explains itself to anyone wishing to follow this path.

Nature is Divine

A majority of Wiccans will tell you that nature is divine. It is like a backbone to the entire practice and there are so many ways that this core belief manifests itself in these rituals. We are all members of this Earth: every rock, tree, leaf, plant, animal, bird, insect, and person, not to mention hundreds of thousands of other species and landscapes.

The Earth is or sacred home and we are a sacred part of it. It is where all life energy is stored and recreated and we are a part of those cycles and systems. To worship nature is to worship the very essence of all things. And you will find that all Wiccan holidays and festivals that are celebrated are derived from the worship of nature.

Each festival is marked by a solstice or equinox. All esbats are marked by the cycle of the moon. And just about every ingredient in the rituals and spells of these festivities comes from nature somehow.

There is also a celebration like the unity of opposing forces. There is always a balance of the light and the dark and nature-worship provide the opportunity to look at life from that place of balance and serenity. It is the presence of the male and female in all things; the yin and the yang. That is nature.

The practice of devoting space and love to nature is a part of the Wiccan creed and even though it is not a demand that you follow that practice, it comes naturally when you consider all of the other core beliefs.

Many of the tools that you will use for your rituals and spells are derived from nature. You will find yourself gathering herbs or pieces of wood for making a wand. You may be harvesting certain plants to hang around your house for a certain holiday, or dressing your altar in the perfumes and trinkets of the forest floor. All of nature comes into Wicca and it is a powerful process to fully connect with the divine in nature.

Karma, The Afterlife and Reincarnation

Karma is an echo of what you may find in the Threefold Law (see below) which states that what you do in this life carries over into your next one. To make such a suggestion, one must believe in the concept of reincarnation, which creates an open doorway for your spiritual being and essence to return to another life, after your last one, to continue to learn lessons and acquire knowledge for the evolution of all things.

According to Wicca, this is what will always be and has always been, and so to adopt the principles of Wicca, you must look into the reality of who you were before, and who you are going to be next. It might be that you are already familiar with some of your past life experiences and you already know what lessons you are trying to learn from those lives. In other cases, for some, you gain new knowledge as you go and are not always privy to what you are supposed to be learning.

The concept of Karma asks that you remind yourself what you need to heal from your former lives so that you can ascend further into your true power and magic. And while you are at it, in this life you are living now, be sure that what you do is something you want to take with you into the next life. This also pertains to the Wiccan Rede 'harm none' (see below).

Although there is the concept of reincarnation, there is also the concept of the afterlife, sometimes referred to as Summerland, and it is here that you rest between lives to prepare for the next one, to gather your strength and reflect on the journey before to create the best journey forward.

All of these concepts help the Wiccan to bridge the gap between Earth and Spirit and that the balance of the divine is always present, no matter what life you are living, or what stage of travel you are in between worlds.

Ancestors

It is not uncommon to call upon the ancestors in the practice of Wiccan rituals and casting. Many Wiccans believe that our ancestors are always with us, guiding us and showing us the way and should be honored for their commitment to forging ahead and living life.

Wiccans celebrate deities of various kinds and it is normal to include your ancestors in your practice just as frequently, as they are a part of the cycle of the self and have many lessons to teach as you grow and honor your path. The concept of honoring the ancestors in not specific to Wicca and is a cross-cultural truth, present in most religious practices.

A great deal of worship for the ancestors comes from a need to embrace the past as well as what your ancestors continue to do for you in the future.

Wheel of the Year

All of the cycles of the year are celebrated in Wicca. Every solstice has a celebration or Sabbat, and every equinox, too. The rituals and spells that accompany these times are a sacred honoring and celebration committed to the end of something to hail the beginning of something new. In the calendar of the year, some endless deaths and rebirths can occur and as a Wiccan, you will find harmony and abundance with every passing season because of that very truth: life begets death which begets more life.

In all of the seasons, there are also moon cycles that are celebrated throughout the ritual of Esbats. The cycles of the moon organize the seasons and every waning moon leads to an ending, into a darkening, while every waxing moon leads to a powerful fullness that has its magic and ritual associated with it.

All of the rhythms and cycles are a part of Wiccan work and it will be a part of this world forever. The concept of worshiping the divine in nature goes closely with the wheel of the year and should be counted as a major component of Wiccan worship.

Personal Responsibility and Responsibility

This concept agrees with the Wiccan Rede and the Threefold Law. You are responsible for every action you take. Wicca asks that you are wise to your power because it might be more than you realize, especially when you are working with the sacred divine energies of all things and all life.

25

When you are practicing Wicca, you are becoming responsible for more than just yourself; you are using the energy of all life to celebrate and support the life you lead and everything you choose can have an impact on another. It is a wonderful way for you to be honest with the truth of karma as well because whatever you are responsible for in this life, goes with you forward into the next.

You are incredibly powerful, and Wicca helps you to embrace your internal power and life force energy; it also asks you to be responsible with your power and to harm none and do right by your actions and rituals.

Benefits of Wicca

Becoming a Wiccan means that you are dedicating your life to being a more positive and focused person. It means that you want to develop strategies to take care of yourself and understand how to be one with nature and everything that exists around you.

It's not just about magical spells or creating potions, but rather wanting self-improvement. There are many benefits to being Wiccan. Wicca and witchcraft emphasized using energy from the earth and nature and also bringing the sky and air energy back into the earth. Being a Wiccan is about feeling as though you are one with the earth, with all living things surrounding and embracing you. It's a peaceful religion.

People who are not Wiccan or do not follow the Wiccan Rede are concerned with control, power, and domination of the earth.

They don't think about living things and they don't care to. They want money and materialistic things to make themselves happy and feel good. This type of mindset is destructive and is one of the reasons that when someone has everything, they still feel as though they have nothing. Most people feel as though when they get everything they want, they will be happy, yet there are Wiccans or non-Wiccans like Buddhists that have nothing and are happy.

This is because they have taken care of themselves and worked on who they want to be for themselves. They view the world as a matter of all living things being one, and they are happy with themselves.

They are at peace with the world and try to give back or give to others as much as possible because they have a sense of well-being. Acting in this way is what it means to be Wicca.

The main aspects of Wicca are what will save the world from human destruction:

- Environmentally friendly people - Aware of the earth. (What affects one thing, will affect all of us, as whatever we do will come back to us three-fold.)
- Responsibility - Your words and actions are no one else's fault, even if it feels like they are.
- Honoring our gods and goddesses which make up all matter and all living things.
- Self-respect, and respect for others.

If everyone lived by these principles, the world would be a much happier place. Nature would live on to survive for centuries more.

All living things would grow and flourish into a beautiful place where they want to be. There would be fewer problems and more help from our society. This is why Wicca is so beneficial.

Wicca is about improving oneself to feel beneficial to the community and their religion. Wicca teaches self-empowerment while offering others the support they need to feel good in their lives too. The wisest thing a Wiccan lives by is as follows: *"If it harms none, do as you will."* This means that you can do as you please as long as you are not harming Earth or anything or anyone around you. Wicca is more about keeping to yourself while focusing on your happiness and goals and avoiding trying to convert others or getting them to see your side. Just live, forgive, and let go. Some of the greatest things about Wicca are as follows:

Wicca is not judgmental. It honors and worships divine femininity; everyone is neither male nor female because everyone is seen as equal and as one. The goddess is the center of everything while the masculine traditions offer accomplishments of the sacred gods - Horned God and the Green Man.

Wicca is nature and Earth-friendly. Wiccans believe that Earth is part of us, and we are part of the earth and all it has to offer. They celebrate food and the gods and goddesses for providing us with all we have, as many cultures are less fortunate. Wiccans have an undeniable connection to all life on Earth.

Wicca honors the physical. The body, the mind, the soul, food, sex, and the physical aspects of the world are all seen as sacred to Wiccans.

Wicca demands creative independence. When someone has come up with an idea for the religion, Wicca is too quick to put that into the religion itself. Everyone is open to their creativity, and nothing is set in stone. Wicca has a strong need for poetry, songs, art, inner experiences, etc. It leaves room for mistakes and does not judge anyone for their past or for who they are today. It's about self-love and inner peace.

Wicca cultivates family time and close bonding. The celebrations like Easter and Christmas are traditional in the fact that they bring families together and help them bond better. Thanksgiving is about appreciation for one another and about giving back to others. Wicca is not a dark religion, nor is it moralistic.

When they hear the name Wicca, right away, many people think about magical spells and Witchcraft. These are the people that don't know much about Wicca and judge based on what's said or what they have heard. Although Witchcraft is part of the Wicca religion, as you have read, it is not everything; however, there are many benefits to the Witchcraft side of things as well.

The Benefits of Witchcraft

No two people, or rather witches, are alike, and no two spells are the same. Witchcraft is all about the energy you put into your spells or potions and not the physical kind of energy. Wiccans are usually light witches and don't practice dark magick due to the law they stand by, which is to harm none. Here are eleven benefits to practicing Witchcraft:

Anyone can become a witch. People from all religions, backgrounds, and cultures can practice magick. Wicca is not the only religion that practices it, nor is it the only reason people will do Witchcraft. However, the reason most people think of Wiccans as witches or warlocks is that they are the most in religion that does practice Witchcraft.

No rules. As with anything or how most things should be in your life, you hold all the control. You can choose to make your spells; do your research about how to carry out certain things like protection spells or healing spells. However, you can make your Witchcraft as simple or as dynamic as you would like.

There are spellbooks and grimoires out there to help you, there are also guides and tools for you to mix when learning. Whatever you do though, be careful in how you use your energy because that is the main ingredient. When you are calm and peaceful, your spell will always turn out the way you would like it to. It also doesn't matter about the lunar phases on when your spell will become successful or when you should start. Wiccans use the lunar phases as a guide to doing their thing.

Anytime and anyplace. When you get good at Witchcraft, you can make up a spell or chant inside your head anywhere you would like at any given time you feel is appropriate. Wiccans and other witches have designated and sacred places to perform their spells and magick. But the choice is up to you on where you would like to learn, create, and spellbinding.

Nature spending. A ton of spells require certain herbs and also things you may have not heard of before, and so you will be spending a lot of time in nature learning about the balance of the earth. With practice, you will learn how to ask for permission and be able to hear the wind or feel the trees and soil beneath your feet. Witchcraft is about being aware of your surroundings, developing a strong mind through meditation, and understanding respect for all living things that involve your environment. There is no better place to get peace other than by yourself in a natural setting.

Knowledge. If you want to do something right or get something perfect, you will have a lot of studying to do. You will find yourself learning about herbs, flowers, roots, teas, potions, spells, and things you didn't think were possible. You will gain knowledge about natural healing, chakra healing, meditation, gems, crystals, myths, history, and the magical properties that every living thing holds. The more you know, the more powerful you will become, and the better off you and your Witchcraft will be.

Knowing what you want. If you are unsure about your passions or your journey as you truck through life, Witchcraft can show you and teach you things you never knew about yourself.

Spell work requires you to have a clear state of mind and a peaceful presence, and so when you do your spells, you have to make sure you are clear on what you want to happen here. As a successful process, doing spells and learning more about Witchcraft will give you insight on yourself and how to reach your most desired goals.

Destressor. Practicing Witchcraft is a time where you can focus your mind on what you are doing rather than all the other things life is trying to throw at you. It creates stability within your brain and your soul spirit. Witchcraft helps you reflect on what you have done, and where you are now for the sole purpose of getting your spell right and having it become successful. If your mind is cluttered, so will your spells.

So many paths to choose from. There are many witches including the sea witch, a hedgewitch, a green witch, etc. Each witch has their unique specialties and practices their Witchcraft a certain way. With the many witches or choices you have, you can find one that you can relate to with the most, and go that path. Or you can choose all the paths and see what kind of witch you will be in a few years. The options are endless, and the choice is all yours.

Excuse celebrating. The summer and winter solstices are one of the many reasons a witch or warlock will choose to celebrate. For example, at the winter solstice, you may have chosen to be a sea witch (works with water), and create spells to replenish the Earth or soil in the dead months. The many Sabbats are easily celebrated, and no witch misses an opportunity to do their traditional rituals. These rituals may include preparing a feast with certain herbs and natural ingredients, go on nature walks to clear their minds, meditation to open their spirit, honor their ancestors for guidance, and many more.

Inclusive. Witchcraft can be anyone, it doesn't matter if you are bisexual, transexual, masculine, or feminine. This culture or religion surrounding Wicca is very "everybody friendly." No witch or warlock feels the need to judge, but they will feel the need to support and encourage. It allows people to try whatever they have wanted for so long and also promotes kindness, self-love, balance, and internal healing.

Increases healthy habits. Because Witchcraft uses everything natural, the teas they drink, the food they make, and a lot of time that they spend outdoors promote healthy habits physically and mentally. Witches spend their free time journaling their adventure, reflecting upon others and themselves, connecting with elements, and taking care of the Earth. They don't make excuses for why they can't do something, and when they have hurt someone unintentionally, they try to express themselves in a way that decreases the conflict.

The bottom line about the many benefits of Witchcraft is that in reality, your main practice is being in touch with yourself while being completely connected to Earth. It's about learning more about yourself and overcoming those unhealthy habits to set yourself up toward your goals. By reading and researching Witchcraft, you may come across many spells and techniques that are most comfortable with what you connect to.

By going this route, you won't be let d, or find any disadvantages, as Witchcraft is about making mistakes, and then gaining rewards and success from learning from your mistakes.

It is an empowering path to choose. With these many benefits comes the power of the mind. With nature comes the health of mental illness. Anxiety is released and mood swings dissipate.

As long as you continue to strive for yourself, you will succeed in whichever path you choose.

How to Deal with the Public If They Don't Accept Your Faith

A lot of times, people will judge the unknown or what they don't understand. They may see you as weird or idiotic because you believe in the magick of Wicca. The thing about this religion though, is that as it is helping you feel more empowered, it will also help you with your self-esteem. When your emotions and mind are in check, what others say you can and cannot do is none of their business. There are two ways to go about your faith in Wicca, both are for several reasons. One way is that you could hide your faith, put your Wicca books away, and don't tell anyone.

The reason for this is you would be afraid to get fired, lose custody of your children, or be discriminated against for your practices. You may keep silent about your given religion because you don't want to indulge in who other Wiccans are as well and ruin their lives.

However, this could stem from paranoia about your faith and how people would act. The other way is to be proud of your faith, and whatever happens, will happen. You may choose to bring out those books, display your gems and crystals, and give advice or support to those who are d the same path as you. Choosing this route is a freer way to be.

Some things to keep in mind is to never ask someone about their religion if they are a Wiccan, some people may find it offensive, and feel judged. If they bring it up, you can show that you are open-minded to the idea, and even ask questions about it.

Also, if you happen to overhear someone's thoughts or faith about Wicca, never indulge or "out" them to anyone else, as it is never anyone else's business. It shows respect for the opposing party as well because you don't know if they want to hide it or if they don't care.

In addition to keeping Wicca a secret, many people choose this route because the person likes to preserve their power and energy, and also Witchcraft should be taught by another person, not by the public. This is because Witchcraft should never be used for the intent to harm, and a true Wiccan will know the intent of someone else while teaching them magic. The people who choose to share their faith openly have their reasons because it shows personal empowerment, and courage stemming from physical, mental, and emotional strength.

Some Wiccans may feel that hiding their faith goes against the religion itself which makes them feel limited to what they can and cannot do. When you are honest about your faith and open to the possibilities, your craftiness becomes more effective, and you will develop self-confidence on a level you didn't have before.

However, most Wiccans choose both sides, they share their faith with close friends and family but don't openly admit it to the world. Whatever suits you and your needs best is your choice, as there is not a wrong choice in this.

As you read, research, and study about Wicca and Witchcraft, be aware that before you choose any route, you should get all your facts right. Generally speaking, elder Wiccans suggest that newcomers should practice, and dive into this religion for about a year before disclosing any information about it.

Find out what suits you, find out what makes you happy, and what you do and do not like. That way, by the end of the year, you will have a better understanding, have more experience, and feel more comfortable about how you will come out about your religion.

Maybe try a bunch of different religions within a few years before choosing what fits you best.

Types of Witchcraft

Just like how Christianity has its denominations in the form of Roman Catholic, Methodist, Anglican, and others, so too does Witchcraft have its set of denominations. Let us look at some of the different kinds of Witches below.

Gardnerian

As the name suggests, these Witches follow the teachings and philosophy established by Dr. Gerald Gardner. In this system of belief, witches practice the religion through a hierarchical system.

At the top, you have the high priest or priestess, followed by many initiates. To become part of the Gardnerian tradition, newcomers have to learn the traditions of the Witch, and then they should have gone through the right initiation process.

Alexandrian

Alexandrian witches follow their system of beliefs and practices. They also have their unique system of initiation and apart from sympathetic magic, they also make use of ceremonial magic. Alexandrian witches also make use of the Qabalah.

Solitary

As the name suggests, solitary witches are those who are not part of a coven. They prefer to practice Witchcraft and perform rituals by themselves. People might choose to be solitary witches either by their choice or because they were never initiated into any coven. Additionally, Solitary witches may incorporate the principles of different Witchcraft traditions (such as Gardnerian and Alexandrian) or they might not use any of the traditional beliefs and rather forge their path.

Eclectic

A Witch becomes Eclectic when he or she pulls from different traditions and belief systems to create the rituals and spells that he or she practices. Their witchcraft practice is more personalized as it involves the traditions of various cultures.

Their system of witchcraft is also prone to change or evolution as they incorporate new ideas and practices.

Traditional

When someone looks back into history and tries to draw inspiration from it, then that witch becomes traditional by nature.

These witches look at old grimoires, historical backgrounds and accounts, and lore to create their practices and rituals.

Because the history of Witches is different in various regions of the world, so are the type of Traditional witches based on the location they practice their craft in.

Hereditary

These are witches who have received their lessons, beliefs, and rituals from previous generations. Usually, these witches are born into a family of witches who has been practicing the art for some time. However, a common misconception here is that just because someone is born into a family of witches, he or she automatically becomes more powerful than other witches.

That is not true. We are talking about Witchcraft, not the X-Men.

Kitchen

A Kitchen witch is not one who has a large cauldron in the kitchen. Rather, they are a group of witches who turn their homes into a sacred place. Kitchen witches enjoy incorporating rituals into their cooking. They focus their energy on the food that they create.

These witches usually grow their vegetables and herbs. To them, the art of cooking is precious, and they care deeply about the meals that they prepare.

Cosmic

When Witches incorporate astronomy and astrology into their workings, they become know as Cosmic witches. These Witches closely follow the alignment of the stars and planets.

They heavily study the symbolism of the various astral bodies present in our solar system and beyond.

Green

You might have guessed as to what "green" refers to. In essence, Green witches work closely with nature. This does not mean that other witches do not have any relationship with nature.

Simply put, Green witches use the seasons and natural ingredients to create their magical accouterments. They also prefer to perform their rituals in the presence of nature as much as possible.

Hedge

One of the special traits of Hedge witches is that they work with the spirit realm. They often create a boundary called "hedge" that separates the real world from the spirit realm. This hedge is a physical border, usually placed around a particular location or their house. To enter the spirit realm, they simply have to exit the hedge.

Common myths and misconceptions surrounding Wicca and witchcraft

Flying broomsticks? Old ladies with green skin? Evil cackling laughter? Hansel and Gretel?

All myths.

And there are more. As we have seen, the church was responsible for spreading much of the rumors surrounding Witchcraft and you know what happens with rumors: they begin to take on a life of theirs.

It's like a game of Chinese whispers. You whisper something to a person and ask them to pass on the information d the line. What the last person will hear may not resemble the original message at all. So, it might have started with an account by some person saying, "They leap into the air on broomsticks!"

That eventually turned to a proclamation that Witches "Fly into the air using broomsticks!"

We all know where that went. And so, in similar ways, much of the myth that you hear about Witches and Wicca is simply bl out of proportion. As in, way out of proportion to a point where you don't even know what the original shape was. So, let us look at some of the myths of Wicca.

Witches Are generally Evil

Let us begin with the mother and father of all myths: that Witches are generally evil.

Let's straighten this out if we haven't already. Witchcraft is one of the most peaceful religions you are ever going to encounter, and that's not because I am writing this book.

One of the main reasons that people use the term Wicca instead of Witch is because of the degree to which Witches were ostracized, attacked, and condemned. Imagine that. You are condemned to such a degree that you decide to rename your identity and belief.

One of the important facts to note about Witchcraft is that it condemns violence and harm done to other people.

Wicca Is Ancient

While the theories, rituals, practices, and principles that guide Wicca are ancient indeed, the entire system was a recent creation.

It started with the Father of Wicca, Dr. Gerald Gardner himself.

He combined both folklore and traditions with modern belief systems to create a whole new set of practices, rituals, and beliefs.

Wicca Is Not a Religion

The United States courts declared Wicca as a region in 1986.

Witchcraft is Satanism

Not even close. When people began to choose apostasy (the act of leaving a particular religion) to worship the Devil, the church blamed Witchcraft for the situation.

If you had to compare Wicca to any religion, then you can compare it to Hinduism for the sole fact that it involves numerous deities.

Wiccans Sacrifice Animals

That is the opposite of what Witches and Wiccans believe in.

Witchcraft respects nature and everything else that is offered by nature. This includes both the flora and the fauna. Plants, flowers, insects, animals, and even the soil beneath our feet are considered sacred by the Wicca.

While it is true that Wiccans make offering to their deities, these offerings are generally in the form of bread, wine, special scented candles, minerals, and other non-meaty items.

Wiccans Have a Dark Bible

The Book of Shadows is not a Dark Bible!

It is simply a collection of rituals that the Witches put together along with other information that they think is important for them to remember. It is a ritual book and a reference guide all put together.

If you had to make it simple, then the Book of Shadows is a journal for Witches.

Chapter 2

Wicca in our modern world

With the creation of various rituals — whether they were for fertility, for growing crops, for success in hunting, or better weather conditions — there arose a necessity for someone to conduct the rituals. This individual would be well-versed about the beliefs, deities, and requirements of the tribes.

These individuals were thought to bring better results when conducting rituals.

Dr. Murray had the belief that in many areas of Europe, these priests became widely known as the "Wise Ones" or Wicca.

Although this statement is often debated (not the fact some priests were called Wicca but about how widespread the name Wicca was initially), what is know is that in many Anglo-Saxon kingdoms, kings and rulers would not make important decisions without consulting with the Witan (derived from the name Wiccan, used to refer to a single wise person where Wicca denoted a whole group of people).

The Witan was labeled the "Council of Wise Ones."

Eventually, the level of importance of the Wicca began to rise. These priests had to have a thorough knowledge of not just magick, lore, and divination, but also of history, medicine, and politics.

They were not just priests, but close advisors to the king. In other words, a mere whisper of suggestion into the ears of kings could send two factions into a state of war. Indeed, priests began to hold considerable power.

To the general public, the Wicca were the mouthpieces of the gods. But when it came to performing rituals, the same Wicca were considered as equals to gods.

Then Christianity arrived.

The Growth of Christianity

Many people believe that Christianity involved a mass conversion but that was not the case. In fact, during its early stages, Christians came under heavy persecution. Both Jewish and Roman leaders targeted Christianity for numerous reasons.

After a great fire broke out in Rome in the year 64 A.D., the emperor Nero came under heavy criticism. He needed to shift the focus of attention away from himself or risk being deposed (or backstabbed by someone you know. It was Rome after all).

He found the perfect scapegoat in Christianity. What made his campaign of targeting the young religion even more successful was the fact that back then people already harbored a misconception about Christianity. Many Christian rituals were thought to include acts of cannibalism. Others were considered to encourage incest.

The stage was practically set for anyone who wanted to blame Christianity for some calamity like, say, a great fire. Through such events, Christianity had slow growth, but it still found a way to spread vastly.

Eventually, an attempt was made by Pope Gregory the Great to mass convert people. To make this happen, he made the people build churches in the same spot that older temples and places of worship were established. It was as though the old religions were being removed and over by Christianity.

However, the pope did not exactly receive the results that he wanted. You see, people were not as gullible or as open-minded to the presence of a new religion as he had hoped. During the time of the construction of the first Christian church, the only stonemasons, artisans, and labor available were people who were "pagans," a term referring to anyone who practiced a religion that was not Christianity. While decorating the churches, these pagan workers added symbols and designs of their religion into the structure. These little additions were done cleverly, in a manner that would escape the scrutiny of Christian priests.

But since Christianity was slowly growing, Wicca and other pagan religions were its opposition. There are, of course, many ways to get rid of opposition. You could sit d and have a proper conversation. You could discuss various logical steps that each party can take to ensure the harmonious existence of both entities.

Or you could do what the Christians did: turn the belief systems of the opposition into something nefarious and sinister.

The church focused its efforts on shifting the perspective of the people about the so-called "Old Religions" (a.k.a. Wicca and other pagan beliefs). Their main focus was to show that these Old Religions worshipped the devil. Hence, the very image of the Horned God was adopted into Christianity as a symbol of the Devil. Lo and behold! A devil with horns was born (or created, depending on how you look at it).

When the idea of the Devil became rooted in the practices, a singular, most obvious conclusion was drawn: paganism involved devil-worshipping! Eventually, this idea of the Devil and paganism became a staple of the religion. As the belief endured, so did its ability to permeate into every section of society.

If you were to count the number of movies that showed witches as people who are conjuring demonic presences, haunting the woods (come on, we have "The Blair Witch Project" and its many sequels to prove that), or simply creating mischief to unsuspecting humans and compare that to those movies that show witches as people living in the woods, then you might notice the difference.

Many missionaries and priests in parts of the world have used the rhetoric about pagan worshippers and the Devil.

But I digress. Back to the Horned god.

In those days, during the growth of Christianity, it did not matter what kind of people followed Wicca or whether they lived much happier and fulfilled lives than Christians. As long as they were practicing a faith that did not include Jesus, they were shunned from society or were asked (asked being a polite term) to convert.

The Devil Wears Nada

According to Professor Henry Ansgar Kelly of the University of California, Los Angeles (Biography.com Editors, 2014), the Devil is mentioned just three times in the Old Testament. Even during those appearances, the Devil performs actions that are administered by God. That doesn't seem like the evil king of hell that we all know about.

Here is another fact to consider.

The whole idea of "evil" being attributed to the Devil is a result of a mistranslation. In the original Hebrew version of the Old Testament, the word for the devil was Ha-satan and in the original Greek version of the New Testament, the word used was Diabolos, both words meaning "adversary" or "opponent." There was never any separation of powers when it came to dealing with religion.

Because there was an all-loving and all-good God, there was just the need to create an entity to give the people the idea that their misdeeds are not going to go overlooked. After all, if God decided to suddenly toss people into eternal fires or make them carry boulders forever, then it doesn't sound like the actions of an "all-good and all-forgiving" entity. They needed another manager for that department.

Even the views of monotheism (the idea that there exists only one God) was not developed by Christianity, Judaism, Islam, or any of the religions that we are familiar with. It was an idea born in Ancient Egypt, during the reign of Akhanaten.

The goat was a symbol of the Horned god. Nowadays, anything connected to the Devil or dark arts use the goat as a symbol.

Begone Heathens!

As Christianity grew, the Old Religions began to fade away slowly. Much of the practice of Wicca was conducted in the outskirts of the countries. There were very few people who would openly declare themselves as part of the Wicca belief.

The words "pagan" and "heathen" were then used to describe anyone who practiced the Old Religion, which is not a bad thing.

Surprised? I bet you are thinking that I just went over the edge, that I am about to tell everyone how terrible Wicca is.

Not even close.

You see, the word "pagan" is derived from the Latin word "pagani," which translates to "people who live in the country." Essentially, it was used to refer to Wiccans, Witches, and anyone who practiced the Old Religion.

Additionally, the word "heathen" is also Latin, translating to "one who dwells on the heath." Heath is a word that describes an open and uncultivated land. Some define it as an area that resembles the countryside. The terms were more descriptive of the nature of non-Christians when they were first used. All ideas of the two words being derogatory are a modern construct and quite incorrect.

The Campaign Against Witches

It was not a good time for anyone to believe in anything that did not conform to the ideas of Christianity. There was a spread of an anti-witch smear campaign, mostly propagated by the churches. It did not help that Witches and Wiccans did not practice their religion openly, creating an air of mysticism around them. Additionally, the fact that they included rituals that did not involve just singing hymns and praising the Lord turned them into outcasts.

Everything that the Witches did was used against them.

Witches used to perform rituals of magick to promote fertility and improve crop conditions. The church claimed that it was because of these rituals that women became barren and that crops were not healthy. There was no mention of the idea that if Witches were indeed responsible for the actions they were accused of, then everyone would suffer equally. Anyone who raised the point was silenced immediately under threat of persecution.

One of the rituals performed by the Witches to improve fertility involved participants to head out to the fields during a full moon. They would then use long tools such as poles, pitchforks, and broomsticks and ride these tools like riding toy horses. They would circle the field and chant, asking the gods to grow the crops with much health. The followers would leap as high as possible into the air. The higher they jumped, the taller they wanted the crops to grow. This was a form of sympathetic magick that did not have the noblest of intentions, but a harmless ritual.

To the church; however, this was an opportunity to turn the idea of Witchcraft on itself. According to the church, the Witches were working against the crops to destroy them. They were not leaping into the air, but rather flying on broomsticks and other tools. Surely such actions could only mean that these people were under the influence of the Devil!

Soon, the fear of Witches took hold among the masses. In 1484, Pope Innocent VIII used this fear to persecute Witches openly. It was two years later that two monks, Heinrich (Institoris) Kramer and Jakob Sprenger, wrote a book that dealt with anti-witchery.

The book was named *Malleus Maleficarum*, which translates to The Witch Hammer. Using the acts of Witches to brand them as evil, the book included detailed instructions on how to deal with Witches. At that time, the official censor (an official or a group of officials responsible for looking at works of art and declaring them as too obscene, politically motivated, or harm to society) was the University of Cologne. Upon reading the book, most of the professors decided that they did not want to be involved with the book at all.

Kramer and Sprenger on the other hand decided to use more nefarious actions to get the approval on the book. They forged an approval letter from the university, which essentially said that the work of *Malleus Maleficarum* was approved and even admired by many of the professors.

The result was like bringing a match to a flammable substance. There were mass panic and hysteria. People took to the streets to condemn Witches. Anyone who was even remotely suspected of being involved in rituals was brought to the streets or were turned over to the authorities. A sense of religious fervor and hatred against Witches took form, one that was not based on any rational thinking. This mood spread all over Europe.

For the next 300 years, Witches would be persecuted. No matter what violence was inflicted on Witches, it was deemed acceptable by the church on grounds of "removing evil." In some cases, inhabitants of an entire village were put to death because of the presence of just one or two Witches among them.

In 1586, the Archbishop of Treves had concluded that the local Witches had caused a severe change in the weather, turning it into a freezing winter. By using methods of torture, a "confession" was obtained, which led to the rounding up of more than a hundred men and women. These men and women were then burned to death.

As we had seen, fertility was an important part of Witchcraft. For this reason, certain sexual rites were also enacted by Wiccan. When the Wiccans were brought in front of Christian churches, they were asked to recount these rites in detail, much to the delight and amusement of the judges and members of the court.

In the end, there was never an exact number to account for the people who were hanged, burned, or tortured by the church. But many estimates say that the total number is close to nine million people. Remember that not all of the people who were sent to their deaths were Witches. As the Witch trials spread across the region, it gave opportunities for people to get rid of anyone they harbored a grudge against or simply disliked.

A good example of how innocent people were caught in the persecution can be understood from the famous case of the Witches of Salem, Massachusetts. It was never confirmed whether any of the victims who were put to their death were followers of witchcraft or the Old Religion. Many people were outstanding members of the community and even the local church!

God and Goddess

Wiccans worship their gods and goddesses through critical awareness. They are aware of the following:

- There is only one "source".
- All gods and goddesses represent a variety of faces from the source.
- All living things on Earth are elements of the source.

The Wiccans' deepest loyalty is to their gods and goddesses which is the "one" behind the mask. The one is the thing you form all your devotion to. The most important thing in Wicca is that you *do* worship your gods and goddesses. The first rule in Wicca and the way of your life is in devoting and dedicating all your actions and your awareness to the creator - whatever that may be for you.

In any religion, they all have one thing in common which is to worship their one divine source. In Christianity, it is a higher power, and in Hinduism, they have many gods. In China, they worship the Jade Emperor.

The gods and goddesses are the ones who share their lives with you and with whom you choose to share your journey. In Wicca, the deity is a transformational spiritual practice to perceive the divine as something that lives in every being as every being:

- Your Mother - the Goddess
- Your brother - The God
- Your baby - The Divine
- Your friend - The Source
- Your enemy - The One
- Your cat/pet - All that is
- Your self - The Eternal Light

The list explains that everything around you is your gods and goddesses. When you truly understand that the divinity is none above others is when you can fully begin to worship all that surrounds you. The list above is what the Wiccan deities are.

Chapter 3

The Wiccan holidays of the Wheel of the Year

Wiccans have what is called the "Wheel of the Year", and it is used to mark d all the major solar and lunar events, which are what their holidays are based on. For example, the Sabbats are for celebrating the sun's influence on Earth, which is the seasonal growing cycle. Wiccan Esbats celebrate the moon phases, especially the full moon.

Here is a list of the Wiccan Wheel Year:

Name	Holiday	Earth Event	Date	Occasion
Samhain	Halloween	fifteen' Scorpio	October 31st	Cleansing and releasing. Celebrating the dead. The Pagan new year.
Yule	Christmas	Winter Solstice	December 22nd	Rebirth.
Bridgid	Candlemas	fifteen' Aquarius	February 2nd	Purification, allegiance, and initiation
Eostara	Easter	Spring Equinox	March 21st	Innovation, revitalization, and new beginnings.
Beltane	May Day	fifteen' Taurus	May 1st	Fertility, happiness, and passion that fuels life.
Lithia		Summer Solstice	June 21st	Passage, and planning
Lammas	First Harvest	fifteen' Leo	August 1st	Appreciation, abundance, and fruition.
Mabon	Thanksgiving	Autumn Equinox	September 21st	Giving thanks, thoughtfulness, and expression.

On all these holidays and events, the Wiccan needs to do traditional rituals. Whether you do it in a group setting, in a quiet get-together, or a full-on drama ritual routine, the point is that you do worship and do the ritual. The rituals consist of:

- Honoring the divine in all the elements of life
- Recharging or regenerate your spiritual batteries
- Centering and balancing yourself with Earth's shifting energies.

The Wiccan dates are confusing, but to start a holiday or a "new day", the Wiccan dates start on the previous day at dusk once the sun has gone d. Each coven or witch will have their way of doing things, but most of the time, the holiday starts at sunrise on the date.

Sabbats and Esbats

Sabbats and Esbats are the time for regrowth, birth, or death of something. They are old traditions that have gone on for centuries, and thanks to our ancestors, they are the start of how our world works today. Eight main Sabbats are revolving around the sun; The Wheel of the Year starts like this:

Yule (Winter Solstice)

On December 21st, 22nd, or 23rd, "Yule" - the winter solstice - starts. Normal people would call this Christmas, and it is the longest night of the year. The festivities of Yule originated back to the Norse people for whom this time of year was for feasting, merrymaking, and, depending on what was believed, sacrificing.

The Wiccans celebrate by decorating a tree, caroling, drinking, and spending time with their loved ones. According to Julius Caesar, this was the time of year where the Druids would sacrifice a white bull and collected mistletoe for the celebration.

In Wicca traditions, Yule is celebrated from back in the Celtic legend of the Holly King and the Oak King. The Oak King represents the light of the new year, and the Holly King is the symbol of darkness. The ritual is when the Oak King tries to take over the Holly King.

Imbolc/Oimelc

This holiday falls on February 2nd and is the first of the three festivals when the Earth starts to replenish the goods. Egyptians thought of this holiday as "the Feast of Nut". Nut's birthday fell on

February 2nd and was seen as a mother figure to the sun God Ra according to the book of the dead. Nut took the form of a scarab beetle and, at the dawn of February 2nd, was know as Khepera. Ireland converted to Christianity, and the church allowed them to worship the goddess Brighid because the Irish found it difficult to get rid of their old gods. Brighid is viewed as the woman aspect of the "maiden/mother/crone" cycle in Wicca and Paganism.

The ritual consists of leaving a piece of their clothing outside for Brighid to bless the day before February 2nd. People put out their fire and make sure the ashes are flat and smooth. In the morning, there should be a symbol or sign that Brighid has left behind if she had passed by the campfire that was made.

If the sign is there, Wiccans would then bring their clothes back inside as they would then have protection and healing powers thanks to the blessing of Brighid.

Ostara

Depending on which day the spring equinox falls on, this day starts on March 1st, 2nd, or 23rd. This day is known as the second of the three spring festivals. The word *Ostara* originated from *Eostre,* who is the Germanic goddess of spring. It's the same day as the Christian Easter celebration, and also what we would call Easter, and at this time, the Jewish Passover takes place. This holiday is one of the "new" holidays for Pagans and Wiccans because the Pagan Germans and Celts did not celebrate this holiday.

The March Hare was a symbol of fertility and growth in the medieval cultures in Europe; this is because mating season happens in March for rabbits, and they all come out in the day when they usually only come out at night.

Beltane

The third of the three spring festivals falls on May 1st, and it has been celebrated for centuries. It means that summer is right around the corner. This is when fire rituals happen, and it stems back to the Greco-Roman religions. It is a fertility month, and the Celts honored this date by giving their gods gifts and peace offerings. Their cattle had to walk through the smoke of the balefires for fertility and health blessings. In Wicca, a Beltane ritual involves fertility symbols, including the Maypole dance. The pole consists of flowers and ribbons that are woven by the dancers. By the end of the dance, the ribbons are intricately woven together to form a pretty pattern. May 1st first represents the endless circle of life bringing birth, growth, death, and rebirth to life.

Litha/Midsummer (Summer Solstice)

Depending on which day the summer solstice begins, this day falls on June 21st or 22nd. Many cultures have celebrated this day as the first day of summer, and it is a celebration to balance the light and dark. This day is the longest of the year, and it's when the sun reaches its highest point in the sky. Just as winter solstice had begun, the Oak King and the Holly King take battle again.

The Oak King is seen as the winter to summer solstice ruler, whereas the Holly King is seen as the summer to winter solstice ruler.

Midsummer, or Litha, is a time when Wiccans would light fires on high hilltops to honor the space between heaven and Earth. In other religions, it is a battle between light and dark. On the first day of summer, the Oak King wins the battle for power, but by the end of summer and by the beginning of the winter solstice, the Holly King takes the power back.

Lammas/Lughnasadh

This holiday falls on August 1st, and it is thought to be the celebration of an early harvest. In some religions, this day is used for worshipping Lugh, a Celtic god of craftsmanship. Lammas is the first of three harvest Sabbats and defines the time between late summer and early fall. In modern days, we do not understand the hard work and survival that our ancestors had to undergo. For us, we go to the store to buy bread, and if we run out, we just return to the store. August 1st represents life and death for our ancestors, as they had to make sure that the first grain was cut, and then the wives had to make bread from scratch. A lot of families would starve if the grain was cut too late or too early. This is a day to give thanks and recognition to our ancestors, as they are the reason we have food on our tables today.

Mabon

Mabon is what we call "thanksgiving", and it falls on September 21st or 22nd, depending on the fall equinox. It is a reminder to us that the long days and hot summer weeks are about to end, and the long winter nights are right around the corner.

This is a time when there is an equal amount of light and dark, which is why we give thanks to all that we have to our crops and harvest. We celebrate the gifts of nature and Earth, while at the same time coming to an acceptance that the soil is dying as the days get colder. In many Wiccan religions, this ritual consists of giving food and harvest to those less fortunate.

This time of year is about the celebration of the harvest and kinship, but also about the balance between light and dark, as the darkness of the moon and the light of the sun are equally balanced.

Samhain

In modern times, we call this day Halloween, and it always falls on October 31st. This holiday goes back thousands of years, and it is known as the witch's new year. Witches will contact spirits through a seance because the veil between this world and the Otherworld is at its thinnest. The celebrations begin at dusk on the 31st, and the new year of the Celtics begins on November 1st, basically indicating that the old year has passed and a fresh new year is now beginning. This is because the harvest has been collected, the soil has died, cattle have been brought in from fields, the leaves have all fallen from the trees, and the earth is slowly dying around us.

This time of year is about saying goodbye to the old and starting to make room for what's to come. For some religions, this night is when they remember their ancestors and all that they have done, so they celebrate their memory. The Esbats revolve around the moon's cycles of lunar phases, and in these celebrations, modern Wiccans and Pagans celebrate the festivity with magick and by honoring their gods and goddesses. Covens usually meet once a month on a full moon to do healing magick rituals. All magick ceremonies represent when the moon is at its different stages - for example, full moon, dark moon, last quarter moon, first-quarter moon, and so on. If a Wiccan was to begin a project, they would start at the sight of the new moon and continue their process as the moon goes through the stages within the month. Generally speaking, a new moon to a full moon represents the beginning of things, and a full moon to dark moon is used for the death of things, like getting rid of the negative things from your life.

New Moon Magick

This moon represents new beginnings, and so this is the phase when witches would start a project. Offerings of milk and honey or water and fertilizer for the plants is how the witches would give thanks to their gods. The goddesses associated with this moon are Diana, Astarte, Artemis, and Ana.

Crescent Moon Magick

This crescent moon faces to the west to the gates of rebirth and death. The shape of the moon means the ladle of love, manifestation, and abundance, and it is the symbol of the goddess.

The crescent represents the cup of the goddess' hand, which represents the gathering of information and new ideas. The goddesses worshipped in this moon phase are Aphrodite, Themis, the Celliech, and Tiamat.

First Quarter Moon

This moon represents growth and to build upon. So, when you see this moon, it is the time to put effort into what is holding you back.

Gibbous Moon Magick

This moon is 10-14 days after the new moon and is the perfect time to make the changes you need from the previous moon phase. It's time to either relax and take some time to think and regain energy or put forth energy into what you have been working on.

Full Moon Magick

The full moon allows you to predict the future and to protect yourself and the ones you love. Psychic powers are heightened at this time, and goddesses such as Arianrhod, Danu, Isis, Ashera, and Selene are called upon to come to help you at this time. Creativity is developed, and chances of success in what you are doing are greatly increased.

Last Quarter

If you want to rid yourself of bad habits, decrease illness, and banish negativity, this moon provides you with the strength to do so. The last quarter moon represents the death of something - to banish something from your life.

Dark Moon

This phase is the most appropriate time for dealing with faultiness or anything that is against you. You should call upon the goddesses Kali, the Morrigan, the Calliech, Lilith, and/or Hecate.

The Wiccan Elements

The elements involved with Wicca include air, fire, water, earth, and aether (which is defined as spirit). The elements are used for spells and are connected to every single thing that involves nature.

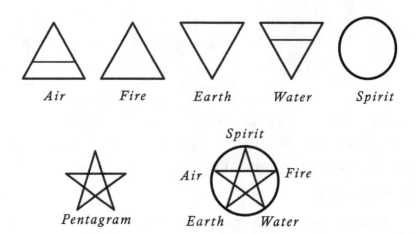

Each witch or practitioner needs to learn about and completely understand the attributes of these elements, which takes time and patience.

Air

In Wiccan magick and rituals, objects are tossed into the wind, aromatherapy is used, songs are sung, and things are hidden in really high places. The spells associated with air involve travel, instruction, freedom, and knowledge, they and can be used to increase psychic powers. Others things air represents are as follows:

The mind and intelligence

- Communication
- Telepathy

- Inspiration
- Motivation
- Imagination
- Creativity
- Dreams and passions

The symbols associated with the air element are the sky, the wind, the breeze, clouds, feathers, breath, vibrations, smoke, plants, herbs, trees, and flowers. The goddesses to call upon when doing air spells are Aradia, Arianrhod, Cardea, Nuit, and Urania; the gods are Enlil, Kheoheva, Merawrim, Shu, and Thoth.

Fire

In Wiccan rituals, witches will burn objects, use love spells, bake ingredients, and light a candle. Fire is the element of change, and it is the most physical and spiritual of the five elements. It represents the following:

- Energy
- Inspiration
- Love
- Passion
- Leadership

The symbols associated with fire are flames, lightning, heated objects such as stones, volcanoes, the sun, the stars, lava, and heat.

The goddesses to call upon are Brigit, Hestia, Pele, and Vesta; the Gods are Agni, Horus, Prometheus, and Vulcan.

Water

In Wiccan rituals, this is associated with pouring water over objects, making potions, healing spells, bathing, and tossing things into a bucket of water. Water represents the following:

- Emotions

- Absorption
- Subconsciousness
- Purification
- Eternal movement
- Wisdom
- Emotional components of love and femininity

The gods and goddesses to call upon are Aphrodite, Isis, Marianne, Dylan, Ea, Osiris, Neptune, and Poseidon.

Earth

In Wiccan rituals, it is common to bury things in the earth, create herbs, and make things out of nature, such as out of wood and stone. It represents the following:

- Strength
- Abundance
- Stability
- Prosperity
- Wealth
- Femininity

Aether (Spirit)

This element is the glue for all the other elements. It provides balance, space, and connection for the other elements. Aether is connected to our sense of spirit and well-being, and it represents joy and union. The goddess to call upon is the Lady, and the god to call upon is the Horned God."

The Wiccan Rede

The Wiccan Rede is what most Wiccans choose to live by. It is a statement that says harm to none, and do what you will. The word "rede" stems back to Middle English and it means advice or counsel.

Chapter 4

An overview of Wiccan covens, circles, and solitary practice

Creating a Circle

A circle is a great way to create personal space for performing rituals. It also protects the Witch from any external influence. As long as you are within the shield, then no negative energy can interrupt your ritual or influence you negatively.

Creating a ritual is not a complicated process. Here are the steps you will need for it.

Step 1

Make sure that you find a quiet place for this. On the other hand, if you already have an altar, you can create a circle around it. If you feel that the circle cannot go around the altar, then you can create a circle in such a way that two points meet at the altar. That way, your altar itself completes the circle for you. You have to be prepared for this process. This means that there should not be any interruptions while performing this process.

Step 2

Find the four cardinal directions using a compass. If you already know them, then skip right ahead to the next step.

Step 3

For each of the directions, place a representation of the elements that they are attuned to. We have already discovered that the north is represented by the earth element. In similar ways, find the elements for each of the four directions. As for what the representation of the elements means, it could be any object that could be symbolic of that element. Here are some examples that you can use:

- Earth: crystals, rocks, branches, potted plants

- Air: incense, feather, a bundle of sage
- Fire: candles, an oil lantern or burner
- Water: bowl or mug of water, seashells

Step 4

Now stand up and look to the east. Ensure that your breathing is calm and steady. If you feel that you might need to meditate before this entire process, then I have provided a simple meditation technique that you can use in the next section. For now, keep your mind calm and grounded in the ritual you are about to perform.

Facing the east, imagine that the wind is blowing all around you. In a clear, but soft voice says, "To the spirits of air, I seek your guidance."

Slowly turn to the south. Imagine the sun above you, throwing its warmth and heat to you. As you can imagine the power of the sun flowing through you, speak these words softly and clearly: "To the spirits of fire, I seek your guidance."

Now turn to the west. Imagine the waves crashing against your feet. Imagine the feel of rain on your body. Imagine how the water feels on your hands. Then speak these words clearly and softly: "To the spirits of water, I seek your guidance."

Turn to the north. Imagine the feel of the earth beneath your feet.

Or imagine the sand slipping through your fingers. Or you could even imagine how the earth feels when you touch it (this might be easy if you have been working with plants or trees). Then speak these words clearly and softly: "To the spirits of earth, I seek your guidance."

Return to the original position.

Note that if your original position was facing any of the directions, then you can come back to it. For example, if you started the ritual by already facing the direction of the east, then you will end up facing that direction. This does not have any influence on the rest of the ritual.

Step 5

Sit d crossed leg or in a position that is comfortable to you and begins meditating. Imagine the power of all the elements flowing into you. From you, they are flowing towards the circle and then powering them.

Step 6

When you are done (ideally, you should have meditated for at least 5 minutes), stand up. You are now going to thank each of the elements for their assistance.

Look to the east and say in a clear voice: "To the spirit of the air, I thank you."

Look to the south and say in a clear voice: "To the spirit of the fire, I thank you."

Look to the west and say in a clear voice: "To the spirit of the water, I thank you."

Look to the north and say in a clear voice: "To the spirit of the earth, I thank you."

Magical techniques like astrology, tarot, runes, and more.

There is a lot to learn about magick, but we will cover them in detail later. For now, I just wanted to give you a short introduction on what magick means in Witchcraft.

The first thing that you should know about magick is that it involves timing. If you have been reading about Witchcraft or of Wiccan beliefs, then you might have read or become aware of the fact that the moon plays a vital role in rituals. This is not a rumor that someone conjured.

The moon is indeed important in Witchcraft rituals. However, the misconception lies in the fact that all rituals are performed at certain times of the year. While the effect of performing rituals under certain moon phases does help in boosting the effects of that spell or ritual, you can perform the ritual or cast a spell at any time during the year. On the other hand, certain rituals are made specifically for certain phases of the moon.

Essentially, there are two main phases of the moon. When the moon shifts from the New Moon stage, go through the First Quarter, and enters the Full Moon stage, then this phase is called the Waxing Moon. When the moon shifts from Full, Last Quarter, and then finally to New Moon, then this phase is called the Waning Moon. Think of it this way, when the Moon is increasing in size, then the phase is referred to as Waxing and when it decreases, it is Waning. These phases are related to sympathetic magick.

You take an object and resemble it to the ritual you would like to cast or the outcome you would like to have. In this case, the Waxing of the moon (increase in size) can be used to improve upon things.

Would you like to improve the opportunities in your life? Would you like to enhance the love that you and your partner feel? Would you like to have more friends? Any ritual or magick that focuses on increasing, enhancing, improving, or other related results uses the Waxing Moon.

On the other hand, you have the Waning moon. If you are aiming to reduce something, then this is the phase that is ideal for the ritual. For example, are you planning to reduce the negativity in your life? Are you planning to remove evil presence? Do you want to manage depression or other health issues? Then you can use this phase.

Each ritual is unique and can be performed during both phases, depending on how you create the ritual or what purpose you would like to achieve. For example, let us say that you have caught a nasty bug. You would like to remove it from your system using Witchcraft. You can do one of the following:

1) If you are in the part of the year where there is Waning Moon, then your ritual should be focused on removing the problem from your body.

2) On the other hand, if you notice a Waxing Moon outside, then you cannot wait for the next phase before conducting the ritual! It's not like the problem is going to take a vacation just so you can prepare yourself! In such scenarios, the alternative would be to *improve* your health. That way, you are simply focusing the ritual on working past the problem and focus on getting you better.

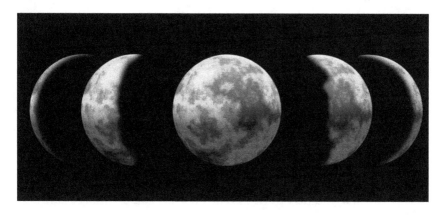

The phases of the moon play an important role in witchcraft rituals

The second factor that you should think about is that magick involves feelings. When you want a magick to occur, then you must be sure about the fact that you want the magick to happen. If you would like to get better, you must want it with all your being. You cannot decide that you are okay with it one way or the other and hope for the ritual to work wonders. It is for this reason that magick is usually performed on the self rather than on someone else. You can control your desires. You can guide the magick to achieve its purpose. On the other hand, controlling someone else's wants is a tricky thing. Your magick might not work effectively on them because they might not want it as bad as you want to perform the ritual. They might have changed their minds or moved on from the problem.

This "feeling" that you have is a sort of "power" for the ritual. You can enhance your power by using chants and rhymes. When you chant or loudly speak a rhyme that you have created, then you are essentially reinforcing the idea of your desires. In similar manners, many Witches also strengthen their spells by performing dance rituals or even having sex. Each one serves a specific purpose, depending on the spell you are casting.

Thirdly, one important note to make here is that when you are performing magick, then you should have a clean body. You have to clean your body both externally and internally before performing rituals. Why? Because you are asking for the favor of a god or goddess. It would be nice to show them that you respect the rituals. Here are the ways you can clean yourself:

1) To clean externally, take a bath with salts (ideally sea salt, but in the absence of that, you can use bath salts or regular salt). If you do not have a bath, then you can take a shower instead. However, make sure you try and use some kind of bath solution if you can get your hands on one.
2) To clean internally, make sure that you have fasted for at least 24 hours before you conduct the ritual. Abstain from the consumption of alcohol, nicotine, and other substances and sex.

Finally, and this is probably more of a guide than a rule. But before you perform any ritual, make sure that you ask yourself this question: Can your actions cause harm to anyone? If they can, then you shouldn't be doing it. No matter what happens.

Meditation and visualization techniques

Too often, you might find yourself plagued by numerous thoughts. When you are in such a state, you might find it difficult to attain a level of clarity. For such situations, here is a meditative technique that you can use. Firstly, find yourself a quiet place where you won't be disturbed.

You can either choose to sit cross-legged on the floor, sit on a chair, or simply lie d on the bed or a surface that is comfortable to you.

- When you are ready, close your eyes and take in a few deep breaths. You could use the counting technique to keep your breaths even and make sure that the time you take to exhale is longer than the time you take to inhale. So, when you are inhaling, count to five in your mind. Then hold your breath while you count to two. When you finally release, you can count to six or seven, depending on how long you take to exhale.
- Once you have taken a few deep breaths, return your breathing to normal. Just inhale and exhale. You don't have to hold your breath at this point.
- When you are in this state, you might notice a lot of thoughts struggling to get your attention. It could be a bad memory, a distracting idea, a future engagement, a project, or anything that is trying to wrestle away your attention from your meditation. Do not ignore these thoughts. Simply accept each thought as it comes.
- Let us say that there is a deadline for a particular project, and it begins to nag at your consciousness. Don't push it

away, as it might return later and this time, with much greater force. Accept the thought. Don't think about why it is there. Don't worry about analyzing it or figuring it out. You are simply choosing to accept its presence. Once done, move the thought away and continue your breathing.

- You should be in this state for at least five minutes or until you find your mind in a more relaxed state.
- Once you are relaxed, simply take two or three deep breaths using the counting technique mentioned above and open your eyes.

You can always perform meditation whenever you feel that you might require it. You can do it each time you start a ritual or after you complete a ritual as well. Just a quick tip: if you are finding it difficult to sleep, you can use the above meditation technique to calm your mind.

The Magick of the Witch

Plant Magick

Throughout history, many plants (and I think probably every plant) have been used in Witchcraft to make rituals or in spellcasting. Some plants were discarded whereas others were used widely.

If you follow the concept of green Witchcraft, where plants are heavily used in the rituals, then there is a belief that all plants contain a form of the spirit. This spirit helps guide the ritual along (we had already seen this concept with animals and humans where each living creature has its unique spirit).

Now, why is it that plants do not have one spirit? Why are all plants not classified or managed by the same spirit? Simple. If cats and dogs each have unique spirits and they are two different species of animals, then it goes that plants also have unique spirits based on their species.

One of the things to note here is that you need to ensure you have awakened your inner Witch before using plants. More particularly, you need to follow the step that encourages you to spend more time with nature. This is because by being close to nature, you allow it to connect with you. Think of it like being in a social gathering. You see various groups in front of you.

If you do not mingle with these groups, can you say that you have understood them or know what is happening within a specific group? If you go ahead and join a group, then you get to connect with the members of that group.

You get to converse with them and understand them better. Eventually, you form bonds with the members of the group. The same theory applies here.

If you do not spend time with nature, how can you understand its powers and its essence? How can you connect with it?

When I say nature, I am not saying that you have to be in the middle of the woods. Go and spend time in a garden or your local park. Get potted plants into your home and then spend time with them. Head over to the nearest conservation center or garden your city offers you and spend time there.

There are many ways that you can spend time with nature. The important thing to note is not the "how," but rather "when." Try and make time for nature in your life. It benefits you in more ways than you can imagine.

Trees

In ancient times, the druids used to consider the trees as sacred. many of them performed rituals out in the open, close to the tree of their choice.

With that in mind, trees have their meanings and symbolism. And even though Witches and Wiccans often focus on herbs, it does not mean that trees are not included in rituals at all. Here are some of the magickal uses of trees.

Type of Tree	Magick Use
Ash	In many European cultures, ash is thought of as the World Tree. It is attributed to strength, strength, harmony, intellect, water, and skill. If you would like to create protection around your home or family, then you can plant an ash tree in your backyard or near your home.
Birch	Traditionally, birch was used to make many of the brooms used by Witches. It is attributed to the acts of purifying and cleansing.
Cedar	For non-magickal uses, cedar has been widely used to repel pests and insects throughout the ages. But magickally, cedar has been attributed to harmony, prosperity, spirituality, and the act of purification. You can also encourage abundance into your homes by building a cedar fence.
Elder	Elder is an ancient wood and is also known as "witch wood." Supposedly, people who do not ask for permission from the tree of an elder to use its wood suffer bad luck and misfortune. You have to use the power of threes while asking for permission or in other words, ask the tree three times to use the wood. There is no specific chant that you have to use. You simply phrase your question any way that you want to. For example, you can say: "Elder tree, may I receive permission

	to use your wood?" In the use of magick, elder wood is used for protection and healing.
Hawthorn	The haw translates to "hedge." It has been said that if the hawthorn grows next to ash and an elder tree, then fairies come out to dance among the trees. Magickally, this wood is used.
Maple	Commonly used for making furniture and other decorative items. Additionally, maple has also blessed the many pancakes around the world with sweet maple syrup. In the world of magick, maple is an equally sweet wood as it corresponds to love, health, life, and prosperity. You know, all the warm feelings stuff.
Oak	Oak is a block of strong wood and is used in shipbuilding, homes, doors, and other woodwork. Magickally, oak is linked to courage, protection, good fortune, and long life.
Pine	The smell of pine is often considered as relaxing. You only have to walk in a pine forest to understand what we mean. Pine is often used in the manufacturing of cleaning products and soap to give that earthly scent. Magickally, pine is associated with healing prosperity and protection from negative influences or spirits.
Rowan	Another wood that falls under the label of "witch wood," is rowan, which is a favorite among Witches, especially in creating wands. Rowan is popularly known to have magickal effects like healing, divination, protecting the user from evil, and improving psychic powers.
Willow	Willow is often connected to the goddess and feminine form. This is why it is preferred in those covens where the sole deity worshipped is the goddess. Magickally, the willow is known to bring about harmony, protection, love, and renewal.
Yew	One must be careful while handling this wood as it is poisonous. It is perhaps for this reason that the yew is associated with death. But while other traditions and cultures consider death as a grim subject to handling, Witchcraft simply acknowledges it as another step towards reincarnation. It is the end of one cycle and the beginning of another. Magickally, yew is connected to the spirit world.

If you had noticed, you were required to ask the elder tree permission three times before you could use it. While this might seem like a rule to follow for one tree, I recommend that you use this rule to pay respect to every tree you come across.

Not only does this ritual allow you to get the full power of the tree, but it also prevents misfortune affect you.

Why would you receive misfortune if you have not done anything evil?

Think of it this way. If someone comes to your home, sits d at your dinner table, and enjoys your incredibly delicious and aesthetically pleasing lasagna, then the least they can offer in return is their gratitude. Imagine if they eat and simply leave your home without saying a single word.

You might not appreciate the gesture, even though you're willing to not make a big deal out of it. While nature is more forgiving and loving, it is still your responsibility to show your kindness in return.

Flowers

Flowers are essentially the sex organs of the plants. This makes it fertile and blessed by the goddess. As such, a flower contains a tiny bit of the goddess' energy within itself.

Flowers are an important component of natural magic. However, they can also be used in other rituals to decorate your altar or to create your spells. Here are some flowers that you need to know about and what they symbolize.

Type of Flower	Magick Use
Carnation	This flower possesses healing energy and can be given to those who are sick or recuperating from some injury. Magickally, carnations are attributed to luck, energy, strength, healing, and protection.
Daffodil	You can use this flower to make charms, especially for your loved ones. This is why, daffodils are magickally attached to luck, fertility, and love.
Gardenia	Another flower that is used in a talisman of love or alternatively. You can use it as a healing charm. Magickally, it is used in healing, tranquility, and love.
Hyacinth	These flowers possess a wonderful scent and are often used in homes. Magickally, they are associated with protection and happiness.
Iris	Witches often use this flower to attract blessings and to purify their spaces. Magickally, they are attributed to harmony and peace in relationships.
Jasmine	Often used in meditative rituals and as a scent, magickally, these flowers attributed to prosperity, spirituality, and love.
Lavender	The aroma of lavender calms the mind, body, and soul. It is often used to bring sleep to those who have difficulty finding it. Magickally, lavender is associated with healing, peace, and tranquility.
Rose	The flower of love! If one does not know what flowers to get during Valentine's Day, then the rose is the fallback option. While folklore (and fiction of course) has popularized the rose as a symbol of love, it has many more uses in magick as it is associated with peace, divination, healing, and spiritual growth.
Sunflower	Because the sunflower is associated with the sun, it is a symbol of vitality and good health. Magickally, it is attributed to success, happiness, and of course, health.
Tulip	Tulips are made to attract abundance and prosperity. This flower is associated with love, money, and happiness.

Violet	You can combine violet with another flower such as lavender and place in under the pillows of children to keep the nightmares away from them. Magickally, these flowers are associated with fertility, luck, love, and peace.

Herbs

Herbs are used in abundance in Witchcraft rituals and spells.

Even if trees and flowers are not used as much, herbs are one of the essential ingredients in Witchcraft.

Here are some herbs that you should know about and their magickal properties.

Type of Herb	Magick Use
Allspice	Allspice is commonly used in cooking and is an important part of a kitchen spice collection. Magickally, this spice is attributed to healing, love, and luck.
Basil	Basil is used heavily in cooking to not only add a slight flavor but an incredible aroma. Magickally, basil is attributed to peace, protection, success, and love.
Cinnamon	Cinnamon is a unique spice used in a variety of dishes. Magickally, it is used frequently to make charms and spells for love, vitality, success, and money.
Dill	Dill is also another herb commonly used in cooking. Magickally, it is associated with passion, protection, and prosperity.
Ginger	Ginger is an important spice in cooking. When it comes to magick, it is used to encourage romance, and improve the finances of a person.
Mint	Mint is an easy herb to grow in the garden or your home. When used in magick, it promotes fertility, success, and purification.
Nutmeg	One of the more recommended herbs for solving problems with digestion. Magickally, nutmeg is attributed to money, love, and happiness.
Parsley	During the times of the ancient Greeks, crowns were made out of parsley for victors of various sporting tournaments and other reasons. This herb is commonly attributed to passion, strength, and purification.
Rosemary	One of the more unique uses of this herb is to darken the hair and cure itchy scalps. Magickally, it is attributed to memory, wisdom, and protection.

Sage	This herb is popularly used for protection. However, it has other magick uses such as health, wisdom, and protection.
Yarrow	A common garden herb whose magick properties are attributed to healing, courage, and love.

Crystals and Gemstones

Crystals are also used heavily in Witchcraft not just for performing rituals, but as decorative pieces. You can use them on your altar or create fashionable jewelry. Crystals focus the energy directed at them and help you make use of that energy. Alternatively, they are even considered to store energy. Here are a few crystals and what they are attributed to.

Type of Crystal	Magick Use
Agate	Agate attracts good vibes and helps you manage your money if you are having trouble with that. Magickally, it is attributed to determination and strength.
Amethyst	This gem is used in meditation to help you enter a relaxed state. Magickally, it can be used to enhance your psychic abilities and call for divine assistance.
Bloodstone	One of the reasons people have this stone near them is to attract wealth. However, it has other magickal uses where it can attract courage, success, and good fortune.
Calcite	This gem is available in a variety of colors, allowing you to use it as a decorative piece in numerous ways. Magickally, it is attributed to healing and purification.
Diamond	A popular stone used in weddings and engagement rings and ceremonies. Diamonds are also possessive of magickal properties. It is attributed to courage and strength.
Emerald	Witches have used emeralds in clairvoyance. However, they have magickal properties that allow them to boost love, healing, and strength.
Fluorite	When placed in a room, this crystal helps remove negative energy in the air. Magickally, it is attributed to concentration, mental clarity, and intuition.
Garnet	Back during the Middle Ages, this gem was often kept in person or worn as jewelry to repel demons and evil spirits. Magickally, it is attributed to passion, love, and courage.

Jade	This gem is used to attract prosperity but has other magickal properties where it attracts good health and long life.
Malachite	One of the main features of this gem is that it attracts prosperity. However, magickally, it has many other uses such as attracting healing and then strengthening the connection with nature.
Moonstone	Shamans have used the moonstone to recall dreams. Apart from that incredible ability, this gem has been used to increase intuition, calm emotions, and improve health conditions for females.
Obsidian	In mythology and ancient lore, obsidian was the material used to create scrying mirrors. Remember the witch in Snow White who kept looking into her mirror and asking, "Who's the fairest of them all?" It can be assumed that the mirror was obsidian too. Magickally, it has been attributed to strength, protection, and for removing mental blockages.
Pearl	This gem is considered sacred to numerous goddesses. It is commonly attributed to fertility and creativity.
Ruby	When you want to improve sexuality and love, you keep a ruby around you. However, it has also been known to build courage and calm emotions.
Sapphire	This gem is commonly used to understand signs and omens. However, when it comes to magick, it is attributed to insight and wisdom.
Tourmaline	This stone is available in various colors

Chapter 5

Self-initiation techniques

It isn't enough to just say you are a Wiccan, because there are so many paths to explore, and which journey you choose to undergo is up to you. Many newcomers may become confused with this process because most religions only have one path with strict guides to follow.

No matter which you choose, what you have read up to this point is solely based around the religion, and how it has come about and why it is known for what it is today.

Every Wiccan still share the same views, celebrate the same holidays, and worship the same Gods and Goddesses.

First, you must understand what a coven is. It is a group of witches and warlocks who sometimes come together and are often very closely bonded with one another. Covens gather together to perform rituals, celebrate Sabbats, and practice Witchcraft on Esbats, as well as worship together at ceremonies.

A group of three or more is considered a coven, but most covens try to reach thirteen people. If a coven becomes too large in numbers to be manageable, they often split or break apart. Wiccan covens are generally led by a High Priest and Priestess, or one or the other.

Other covens may have a vote to switch leaders, and everyone inside the coven gets a turn at leadership. So, you have done your research and decided you wanted to become a Wiccan.

You have engaged in all their beliefs and lived by the religion through thick and thin. Eventually, you decide that it's about time to find other Wiccans and join a coven. But how?

This can be a tricky process because much like yourself, other witches or Wiccans have probably kept their faith a secret and shared it with other close relatives or friends. When finding a coven or other witches like yourself, you must use caution. Just like any group or set of people, there are good and bad, in this case, light witches and dark witches. Some use white magic while others use dark magick and will know that you are a newbie.

They may act nice and become your friend, but they intend to use you and steal your power to become stronger themselves.

Do not get the "dark witches" confused with the Wiccan religion. The witches who choose to use dark magick are not classified as Wiccan believers and do not fall under the name Wicca.

With that said, any Wiccan who practices dark magick is not Wiccan at all and are witches who practice black or dark magick.

As stated before, a true Wiccan lives by the following motto: "Harm none, do what you will." If dark magick is used, the witch practicing is not following the only true rule in Wicca.

Here are a few things to keep in mind during your search for others like you.

- Don't be desperate. The more anxious you are to find a coven or a witch the more at risk you are at finding someone who wants to take advantage of you.
- Get to know the opposing party first.
- Find out about their beliefs, what they have practiced in the past, and what drives them the most.
- Ask them about what they expect from you if you decide to join them.
- Do some research about the path these other witches have chosen. Learn the advantages and disadvantages (the goal is to be one step ahead).

- Before joining their coven do a public ritual with them to get familiar with what they do.

If it feels good, seems good, and there is a close bond, then it's probably good.

Although, through your journey of being a Wiccan, you may have experienced a deep intuition. You must always listen to your instincts. If things feel good, then do it but ease into the group and gatherings, never rush. There are some signs of coven cautions in which you should run away from or avoid at all costs.

The last thing you would want is for a dark coven to take your light from you because they seem to know what they are doing.

However, I would like to mention that if you do come across a "dark coven", they are not acting as true Wiccans. It is so important to realize what Wicca stands for and anything that portrays darkness is not Wiccan. Here are some coven warning signs in which you should stay far away from;

- Insists you obey their rules and laws while also telling you what you should think and feel.
- It makes it known that their way is the best and only way, which they claim to have the highest power.
- Demands that you believe what they believe and to forget everything you know
- Gets judgmental or even violent when you try to explore other options and learn from other sources.
- When you question them or their motives, they become angry with you or intimidating.
- Pressures you into doing things you don't believe in or are uncomfortable withSays that you have joined the coven whether you intended to or not.
- Uses magick for dark things like trying to harm people and other living things
- Tries to convince you that dark is better than light.

- You feel as though you are not equal and need to earn your way to the top in their eyes.
- Wants and expects you to recruit others into the coven
- Says things like "I could get in trouble for teaching you this but..." or "No one else knows about this."
- Talks about summoning demons or controlling the Otherworld
- Leaves you with fear, shame, guilt, anxiety, and other negative feelings.

These are just a few signs that you need to be aware of, but mostly pay attention to your intuition and use your head when finding other covens. If something doesn't feel right, most likely it is not.

During your search, it is not just a good thing to watch out for the "bad" covens (non-Wiccan practitioners), but to keep in mind and be aware of the "good" covens as well. When you understand the key differences, you are ready to find what you are looking for.

Most of the time, finding a good mentor or coven is common-sense. Here are signs to watch out for when you have been introduced to a "good" mentor and coven.

- The teacher respects your needs and boundaries
- If the teacher asks you for a small but fair fee to teach you
- If they share their beliefs and interests with you
- They are patient, knowledgeable, and willing to share their expertise
- They are open, upfront, and honest
- If you find a teacher, it should be that they have been practicing for at least five to ten years
- Honor your right to seek out other sources as well
- Do not pressure you into anything
- Usually, leave you feeling confident, empowered, and motivated

- Their knowledge and ways of teaching are encouraging and helpful

A good indication that you have found a good mentor, or coven to join is when they make you feel good about yourself and treat you as an equal. In any case, though, make sure you never give your power to anyone. Ask for the guidance help of your Gods and Goddesses and follow their signs which should lead you to the right people.

Getting back on track to how you can find yourself a coven to join or a mentor to trust there a few steps you need to take to get there. Here are the steps:

Know what you need to look for

The first step is to have a clear vision as to what you need and want. Know what you are looking for before you start looking. Make sure your research is up to date and you are knowledgeable about what to find. A few questions to ask yourself are as follows:

- Do you need a coven? Why?
- What ideals are the most important to you? (look up Wiccan Philosophy for ideas.)
- Why do you want to practice Wicca? What would you use Witchcraft for?
- Why do you want to find others like you? To connect with, to talk to, learn from, or practice with.
- Once you have a clear vision of what you are looking for, you can start

Become an

The second step is to let yourself become on to other witches and covens out there. Let them know you are looking for help, and what kind of help you need. There are a bunch of spells and rituals you can do to "put out a call." After this, let the universe take over, and be patient as you wait for a response.

Take classes

The best way to seek out other witches is that you go into the world and take self-care workshops. Things like how to find what you want. Anxiety and mental health groups are good finds. Also, you may try looking into miscellaneous workshops that seem as if no one would take them but they still interest you.

Be found

The next step is to be found and be upfront about who you are (if you are comfortable). When you identify yourself by wearing Wiccan jewelry, then another witch may spot you and want to reach out. For a more subtle approach, wear things only other Wiccans would know about but that are classy or just unique designs to a normal person.

Seek other Witches

The last step is to find them yourself. Witches are everywhere, but no one knows who they are because they are still very private. The good thing about having practiced Wicca on your terms is that you are experienced enough to know the signs of someone else practicing as well.

- Go to bookstores, and observe what books people are reading. If someone is reading a Wicca book or spell book, then this can be a clue.
- Go to a witchery store, many ts and cities have them. These stores mainly have tarot cards, palmistry teachings, astrology, energy healing, crystals, etc... You may run into someone. Yoga classes are good classes to sign up for. Many people who practice yoga, practice meditation, and

so when you meet someone, they may just open up to you about why.

- Sign up for Witch forums, there is tons of information online and with online witches. Who knows, you may even find an online tutor who can point you in the right direction.

If you decide to give up the search and just start your coven while having others find you then make sure you have done all your research before starting. You wouldn't want to come off as offensive or do things inappropriately because you don't know what you are doing.

If you keep Wicca Spirituality alive throughout your journey to start a coven or find one, you will always have the blessing and guidance of the Lady and the Lord.

Initiation

If you are a newcomer to Wicca and Wiccan beliefs, when joining a coven you may be asking what exactly is initiation? What exactly do you have to do? The reason initiation is crucial is because, for some people, Wicca is just an interest.

Witchcraft and things to do with Wicca seem new and exciting but after a while, they lose interest. Others may just need to be introduced to Wiccan ways so they can discover their true path somewhere else. Then, there are those people who find a sense of peace and belonging to this journey that they have come across and discovered.

This is a way of life for these types of people. So, what is involved in a Wiccan initiation ceremony? First, you must figure out if you want to go solo or if you want a group with you that shares the same beliefs and values as you when it comes to this path.

When we think of the word *initiation,* we imagine some sort of group setting where a person is admitted into a particular organization. If you plan on joining a coven, then this image is almost correct. In Wicca, initiation means to pass d the knowledge of one Wiccan to another. In a coven setting, the leader will pass on their knowledge to the initiated and when the leader feels as though the newcomer is experienced enough to do a ritual or practice on there is when they are ready.

When the leader feels as though the "newbie" is committed to this spiritual path, then this is when they can officially join the Wicca religion or coven.

An initiation is different in every group; however, it is a process where a series of events helps the individual transform spiritually and is dedicated to this life decision. After this step, the individual becomes accepted into the rite itself.

One of the first steps, before initiation begins, is that the individual seeking initiation and the coven itself has to be wholly committed to each other. The individual has to find and be a good fit otherwise, it won't work out.

The initiated has to learn basic information involving the coven ways, history, and traditions to get a sense of whether or not the individual wants to contribute their energy to this coven.

When you do find a good fit, the next step is to work one-on-one with a mentor or leader of the group in which is called the study period.

This stage is when you become vulnerable, and share your beliefs and practices with the leader and vice-versa. Once initiated, it is your responsibility to commit to and honor your vows to the coven. You will vow secrecy, attend meetings, and join every ritual to be a part of the coven membership.

One thing is most important when seeking initiation into a coven or group. If you don't know what you are doing or looking for you should never enter.

Covens take initiation seriously and are willing to share their spiritual and emotional bonds with you while expecting the same. It is crucial that you are completely compatible with the group to avoid conflict of interest.

Most covens are closer to each other than their families, so this is why it is very important to choose the right fit. It would be better to practice on your than become involved and dedicated to a group that is full of conflict and is anything less than supportive and fulfilling.

Solitary Wiccans

A solitary witch or practitioner is someone who chooses to practice witchcraft in the privacy of their home or another place that feels safe to them.

Many solitary witches prefer to experience things on there and it requires self-dedication to their faith and spiritual path.

Although these types of witches do not have a coven, they may participate in the traditions of Wicca like Sabbats (holidays).

Many solitaries are called Neopagans which engage in the Pagan religions that include different forms of Wicca, Traditional Witchcraft, and many others. A solitary witch will teach themselves on the many practices and paths from Wicca.

They will read books, research herbs, and create their spell books. Aside from the many mistakes, one can make without guidance, they are some of the most powerful witches around.

One reason for becoming a solitary Wiccan or Pagan is because the individual does not want to feel judged or have to justify their beliefs to anyone else. They fear that they may set themselves up for harassment or abuse within a group setting.

Another reason for their choice to be solitary is that it is just their preference to practice alone because they feel more comfortable doing so.

With solitary witches, there are no initiation acts, but rather there is self-dedication to their practice and beliefs. The solitaries choose this path because they feel it is right for them, and they don't feel the need to reach out to be initiated because they know what they want. Self-dedication happens when you declare a ritual or practice strictly to yourself and make vows to your deities.

You can call it whatever you like because in a sense it yourself that is fully committing to the religion and all of its practices involved.

You feel as though you are ready, and whatever you have been working on and researching, only you will know when you are fully ready to commit yourself to this path you have chosen. So, whatever you decide to call this "self-initiation" process there are milestones to complete to fully commit.

Firstly, you must become familiar with the Craft - finding out what works for you, which witch you resonate best with, and which traditions feel most important to you.

The recommended time to study and practice this way of life is a year and one full day before self-dedication day. You can take longer, or if you are a natural, you can be shorter, but it must be something you want to do and are fully ready for.

The next step is to figure out what you will do for your ritual. You can find information online or in Wicca books.

Look for information, articles, or books called solitary practitioners for your best results. If you haven't found something you are interested in, then you may need to create your ritual, and by now

- if you are truly ready - you should have enough experience and enough knowledge to design or create something like this for yourself.

Along with your research and pulling some pieces from here and there, when doing your initiation ritual, you may want to ask the guidance of your Gods and Goddesses to help you complete the process.

Initiation whether it is completely on your, or if it is in a coven of your choice, is completely optional. With this in mind, understand that even though this is your choice now, it may and can change later. Some Wiccans have never been initiated and have practiced for years. There are also initiated witches who have lost interest and gone their way.

If this is the life you choose, then you must acknowledge that you have to go at your pace and follow your instincts to become completely successful in this religion.

Forms of Wicca and Wiccan Traditions

Along with the choices you can make about initiation, joining a coven, being completely solitary, or otherwise, there are decisions to make based around Wiccan traditions as well.

There are different types of Wiccans, just like there are different types of witches, which we will get into later. There are six different forms of Wicca and in each type, there are the traditions that they follow as well. Here is a list of the different forms and traditions of Wicca:

Gardnerism

Gardnerism is both a traditional form of Wicca and a family lineage. The original book that was written by Gardener has been passed d, and there have been many versions. But within this Wicca form, the rules, or practices in this book are still preserved.

Gardner is largely responsible for bringing the first craft tradition to life. The Gardnerian Craft is the most familiar when we talk about Wicca and what Wicca stands for.

They hold the same traditions and undergo the same types of initiations; all covens hold a High Priestess or High Priest. They still follow the Wiccan Rede and are perhaps the oldest of the Wicca forms there are.

Alexandrian Wicca

The Alexandrian Wicca holds many aspects similar or the same as Gardnerian Wicca. However, the fire element symbol is an athame, and the symbol for air is a wand.

Alexandrian Wiccas focus mainly on the Holly King and the Oak Kings for several of their rituals and do much magick when celebrating their traditions.

The High Priestess is the highest authority of the coven and is usually a man that leads the group. Alexandrian is a bit different than Gardnerian because this Wicca is more diverse and socially formalized. Gardnerian keeps strict rules to refrain from nudity rituals, whereas Alexandrians leave it optional.

Mary Nesnick was initiated into both coven groups Alexandrian and Gardnerian. She implemented and combined both traditions and rituals into what is called Algard. The only way it was possible is that both forms of Wicca were so similar that it just seemed to work.

Dianic Wicca

The Dianic Craft involves two different branches. One branch was founded in Texas by Morgan McFarland and Mark Roberts. They honor the Horned God as the Goddesses' beloved consort.

The coven is mixed with both females and men and is sometimes referred to or thought of as "Old Dianic." The other branch - branch two - consists of an all women's coven and is sometimes referred to or known as 'Feministic Dianic Witchcraft."

They experiment with different rituals and tend to be loosely structured. This group is supportive of an emotional and personal aspect.

Celtic Wicca (Church of Wicca)

The Celtic Wicca Craft was founded by two men named Gavin and Yvonne Frost. For a while, only the gods were honored and worshiped, but most recently the goddess includes their deity.

Celtic Wicca uses three circles using salt, sulfur, and herbs, whereas other Wiccans only use one circle. Unlike other Wiccans, the Celtic Wiccans insist on using a white-handled athame rather than a black one like everyone else.

The Frosts have gathered courses to teach about the Celtic Wicca and other forms of Wicca, which has been frowned upon but is why they are more public in most of their traditions.

Georgian Wicca

Georgian Wicca is very dynamic and makes room for various styles and creativity. The best name for this group or Craft would be "eclectic." The founder of this Craft is George Patterson, and he used the phrase, *"If it works, use it - if it doesn't, don't."* This means that within the Georgian Wicca, as long as you do not harm, you can create and free your mind with practice whatever you want.

Discordianism (Erisian)

This Wiccan Craft is about orderly with the disorderly. So, in other words, the absurd is just as logical as the mundane, which is just as legitimate as chaos which, in turn, is as valid as of order.

Discordianism brings humor into the equation but should never be taken as a joke. It allows the practitioner to play games with an order, or games with chaos, or even both.

The effects of this craft on an individual can be exhilarating however, they may have missed spiritual growth together when joined with Discordianism.

Whichever path you decide to choose, you will find at least one that resonates best with you and who you are. These Wicca forms are not to define who you are or who you want to be, they are mostly about the history of Wicca and how it came to life.

What's more important is which witch you are planning to be.

There are hundreds of types of witches, and one of them is bound to suit you and your personality. The reason why it should take a year before thinking of being initiated is so that the individual can practice different spells according to each witch, and which suits them best.

Types of Witches

When we think of witches, we think of the old stories with broomsticks and the creation of potions and women cackling under the moon. This is the image of children's books or maybe the media of the old days have led you to think about witches. However, this is not at all the case. The real story is that many types of witches are scattered amongst us. Below are some details regarding most of them:

Alexandrian witch. As we mentioned in 'Alexandrian Wicca,' it was founded by a guy named Alex Sanders and his wife Maxine. This is based on the ways of Gardnerian Wicca, but the main difference is that Alexandrian Wicca combines elements of traditional magick and Qabalah. To become an Alexandrian witch, you must be initiated into a coven and obtain the three levels of Witchcraft.

Augury witch. The word 'augur' is a Roman term that refers to someone who seeks out to find out whether the Gods approve of a specific action taken by an individual. The witches seek this information by translating signs and omens that the individual has experienced on their spiritual journey. An Augury witch is a translator between the universal forces and people on a spiritual quest.

Ceremonial witch. The ceremonial witch does everything by the book. They have vast knowledge about traditions and rituals and most often will have grimoires and spell books.

They might have a book of shadows and draw on their knowledge such as sacred mathematics and quantum mysticism. They call upon archetypal figures and understand spiritual entities that possess the kind of energy the Augura Witch wishes to have.

Dianic witch. This cult or coven focuses solely on worshipping the Goddesses and is more or less a feminist of all Wiccan movements.

The Dianic witch will honor their Goddess through three aspects containing, Maiden, Mother, and Crone. Dianic witches mainly consist of women.

Druid. Druids are perhaps the most secretive of all because there is not a ton of written information about them. Julias Caesar wrote about Druids in his diary *'The Gallic Wars,'* and described them and organized religion with their ways of doing things in rites and rituals.

Neo-Druids take their practices from old sources that originate from the Romanticism Movement of the eighteenth century. Druids worship the Earth mainly revolving around nature, and implement these honors to their Gods through meditation and ceremonies.

Eclectic witch. Eclectic witches do their thing and don't normally follow any religion or Witchcraft practice. Instead, they draw from their 'higher self' and practice rituals or activities that work solely for themselves. Most Eclectic witches have their practices and come up with their creation of rites and rituals that are derived from their research.

Faery witch. Similar to the Eclectic witch, the Faery Witch has its practices as well. The difference, though, is that they tend to have communication with faery folk and nature spirits. Many of their routines or Witchcraft is created from the individual.

Green witch. A green witch will communicate with 'Mother Earth,' by using sacred oak tree groves in their rites and rituals. They do this because it brings them closer to nature and makes them feel closer to the Divine spirit. There are two different green witches in which they both use their materials for their ritual practices.

A Flora Witch will use flowers and flower materials for their rituals. An Herbal witch will use herbs and extractions from plants and minerals for their practices.

Hedgewitch. Just like a Shaman would be able to do, the Hedgewitch can travel to the Otherworld and communicate with the spirit realm. This type of witch is known to be a powerful healer or midwife who specializes in delivering messages into real life to others and vice versa.

The word 'hedge' is a mark of a village or settlement in the old days where the boundary between physical and spiritual worlds was balanced.

Hereditary witch. The hereditary witch is a witch who has been born into a family of witches and brought up by their practices and beliefs. They pass their practices and rituals d to their children for generations.

The child who is born into this Witchcraft religion can still make their choices and only become a Hereditary witch if you accept the practice into your heart.

Kitchen witch. A kitchen witch is not what they seem - brewing potions and cooking with herbs in the kitchen. They use realistic and useful tools to engage in rituals, ceremonies, and magic. The Kitchen Witch enjoys decorating her home with magick and have it be a sacred and safe place to be.

Secular witch. A secular witch will use crystals, herbs, and stones in her practice; however, she does not define these items as divine or spiritual. She believes that the objects she uses for her rituals and witchcraft activity holds energy and does connect to the universe and Earth, but the Secular witch doesn't worship any deities or spirits.

Solitary witch. The Solitary witch doesn't follow any organization or engage with a coven, and they don't belong to any religion or have a correspondence with any set practice. It is said that solitary witches have practiced their craft for many lifetimes, and when they reach puberty, their knowledge is re-awakened.

This means that even though they don't remember being a witch, once they start Witchcraft, their mind does too, and so they are real naturals at it. Thus, they don't need any help from anyone else to perform their magick rites.

Whether you decide to practice Witchcraft on your, follow a coven for help, are already experienced, believe in Wicca, or don't.

The choice is purely up to you. You can be a witch without believing or worshipping any Gods and Goddesses, or you can be a full-fledged Wicca with your beliefs and practices and create a bunch of covens together. The choice is yours, as there is no 'right' or 'wrong' answer.

Awakening the witch within you

To awaken the witch within you, various methods combine both directly calling out to the powers to surrounding yourself with symbolic items.

Call Out to Your Power

Many had silenced the power of the Witches. You are going to call out to these powers. You are going to reach out to the god and goddess to grant you the power that was once taken away from Witches. To do this, find a quiet spot. You can choose to be in front of your altar or you can find any other spot where you won't be disturbed during the ritual. Once you are ready, following the steps below:

- Make a triangular symbol with your hands by touching your thumbs and your index or first fingers.
- Now, slowly bring this symbol close to your abdomen area. Take a deep breath and exhale. You can even perform the deep breathing exercises we had seen in the previous chapter.
- Set your feet apart and relax. Make sure that you are not feeling the tension in any part of your body. If you need time to perform a quick meditation, then you can do so before starting this ritual.
- With your feet apart, bend slightly at the knees. Close your eyes and bring your attention to the region of your third-eye. This region is located in the middle of your forehead, between and slightly above your eyebrows.
- In a clear voice, speak the words, "Oh God and Goddess, grant me the power that was once lost to me." If you have chosen to acknowledge only the goddess or god in your coven or practice, then you can change the chart above. You can say either, "Oh God, grant me the power that was

once lost to me" or "Oh Goddess, grant me the power that was once lost to me." If you prefer, you can even replace the word god or goddess with the name of a specific entity. This allows you to directly connect with a deity.

- You have to repeat the above chant three times.
- Once you have uttered the chant, take a deep breath. Allow the power to manifest within you.
- Then speak this chant out loud three times: "I am deserving of this power."
- Finally, take another deep breath. Once you are done, speak this phrase only once: "Blessed be."
- Now you can relax and return to your original position.

Keep Symbolic Materials

You can always choose to keep crystals or other materials with you. We are going to look at crystals in-depth in the next chapter. But for now, let us look at the way that you can keep crystals with you.

- You can out all your crystals into a bag, especially a small pouch that you can carry around with you. You can either keep this push in your pockets or hand it around your neck.
- You can have a crystal bracelet. You can add as many crystals as you like in your bracelet or simply add multiple stones of the same crystal.
- A pendant is a stylish way to keep your crystal close to you. The best part is that you do not have to hide the pendant at all. You can choose to wear it openly. Some Witches even have different pendants for the various crystal to match their different wardrobes.

Surround Yourself with Nature More

Witchcraft is a religion that is based on nature. So, it would help if you headed out and experienced nature more. This could be anything from taking a walk in the woods or going hiking on a mountain to simply walking along the beach when it is relatively quiet. When you experience nature, you not only empower yourself more but also infuse your mind with positivity and calm.

Be Comfortable with Yourself

When you adopt the identity of a Witch, then any hesitation will diminish the powers that you have. This is because being a Witch means accepting everything about life. When you do, the god or goddess (or both) find it easier to communicate with you.

The best way to think of this is by using the example of swimming. Many people are afraid of dring when they first get started. But the idea is to face your fears and practice anyway. If you decide that you cannot do it and simply choose to avoid practicing swimming, then you will never learn to swim.

The same rule applies here. If you are going to be a Witch, then make sure that you are receptive to the powers of the deities. And that can only happen if you accept yourself and accept them into your life.

Chapter 6

Step by step instructions for constructing a ritual

Rituals take many forms and represent so many different things to a Wiccan, or any person devoting themselves to this kind of magic. Rituals have existed for as long as human beings have, even in their most Neolithic forms. The ritual is a cause to express intentions and devotions through the world of energy, elements, and spiritual connection and as you will notice in your research, every culture throughout history incorporates some kind of ritual practice into their lives.

In Wicca, rituals are about a connection to the divine, spells, crafting, and honoring the deities and rhythms of life. They are specific to each practitioner or coven and can be delivered in a wide range of experiences and formats.

In your Wicca Starter Kit, you will have the step-by-step guide to performing a ritual. Keep in mind that each ritual must be altered and enhanced according to whatever magical purpose you are working with. There may be a lot of ingredients for you to choose from and work with and there could be a lot of steps and degrees, or levels, of practice that you have to go through. It depends on your spell, and whatever steps you are creating through your Book of Shadows and your solitary practice.

If you are in a coven or choosing to become a part of one, many of the rituals performed are already outlined. This book focuses more on the ritual practices involved in a solitary Wiccan.

Let's get started with these basic and simple guidelines to help you picture the process of your ritual work.

Step 1: Preparations

Before any ritual begins, you need to make the proper preparations for it. Preparations can include all or some of the following:

- Scheduling the ritual (Esbats and Sabbats have specific dates. Other rituals may need to fall on a certain date because of numerology, moon and sun cycles, birthdays, etc.)
- Organizing the steps (You will need to decide what order you need to carry out certain components of your ritual based on your knowledge of a spell you are working, or referral to your Book of Shadows. Having the information handy and in your cast circle is an important part of preparing)
- Collecting your ingredients (You will need a variety of items, not including your altar or regular tools, that need to be used for your ritual. This can include specific herbs, crystals, candles, and their colors, types of incense, etc.)
- Bringing all of your tools and ingredients into space (You will need to have all of your collected tools, objects, ingredients spell book, or ritual instructions, and anything else you might need, in the space and ready to work on the chosen day and time)
- Setting boundaries with other life matters (You will need to turn off your cell phone and other distractions and create a time and space with your family and loved ones to give you undisturbed time to practice your ritual)

You may find other preparations outside of what is on this list and that is all dependent upon the specific ritual or spell you are trying to cast.

Step 2: Casting Your Circle

For every ritual that you perform, for the sacred quality and nature of this experience, you will need to cast a Ritual Circle to support the energies you are trying to engage with and focus on.

Follow the steps for Ritual Circle Casting in Chapter 4 to prepare your circle of protection. Make sure that all of your tools, ingredients, and objects needed for your ritual are already inside of the area you will be working in after your circle is cast.

Step 3: Honoring the Gods/Goddesses

Part of the reason people perform a ritual is to honor a sacred deity to their practice. Many Wiccans perform rituals for a specific God or Goddess and honor them regularly through a ritual to help them enforce their energies to work on other magical purposes.

The honoring of a deity or spiritual presence through a ritual is a sacred way to incorporate that presence int your everyday Wicca practice and will help bond you more deeply to the kind of magic you are choosing to practice.

Rituals open your space and your energy to receiving more of the gifts of that divine presence and so after you connect to casting your circle off protection, you begin your words of blessing and prayer to the god or goddess you are calling into your ritual, either to honor them directly as the purpose for the ritual or to include them in whatever other rituals you are working to perform.

Step 4: Tools and Ingredients

At this point in your ritual, you will likely need any tools and ingredients required to perform your ritual. You may have already used some of your tools during the casting of your circle and you will want to be sure to keep the tools you need to use in your ritual instead of using them for placement of the circle.

For example, rather than place your Chalice of water in the west, place a bowl of water there and keep your chalice in the center with you, or on the altar so that you can use it for your ritual.

Whatever herbs and ingredients you need to use can be prepared in whatever fashion they need to be. There are going to be specific instructions according to each ritual or spell and so you will need to have those instructions in the circle with you, to prepare your herbs and essences accordingly.

You will most likely be using your tools and ingredients together to complement each other's energy. This preparation stage can be on your altar or a table or on the floor where you are sitting.

Step 5: Connecting Your Intentions and Invoking Your Purpose

With your tools and ingredients ready to perform magic, you can begin the part of the ritual in which you will charge your tools and ingredients with the intentions and purposes of the ritual you are performing. You have read in Chapter 3 about how to charge and consecrate your tools.

Depending on your spell work and your intentions, you will imbue your ingredients, objects, and tools with that sacred purpose at this stage to prepare for the rest of the ritual. Putting that magical intention into your objects and tools first will only empower your ritual more fully and is an important step in the process.

Be specific and clear and let your intentions and magical purposes invoke the appropriate energy for your ritual.

Step 6: Practicing Magic

With your tools, implements, and ingredients charged and consecrated, you can now begin to practice your ritual magic. This stage will include a wide variety of steps and is entirely dependent on what your Book of shadows says to do, or whatever your spell work instructions might ask of you. Some of these steps can include:

- Lighting the candles specific to your spell (they will already be charged, consecrated and anointed if you followed the last step)
- Burning of certain herbs

- Using your tools in a specific way to invoke and honor specific energies and/or deities.
- Dancing
- Chanting
- Speaking Spell words
- Pouring specific beverages into the chalice to drink and honor a deity or holiday celebration
- Appointing certain elements to aid and guide you through the use of your wand or athame.
- Burning ingredients in your cauldron

There are plenty of other possibilities that will arise with certain rituals and spells. Some, none, or all of these things can occur on your ritual and it will be up to your Book of Shadows and your intuition to build the ritual and the steps involved.

Step 7: The Power of Words

This step will overlap inside of Step 6, as the words that you use for practicing magic will have a powerful impact on your ritual. You may say words during your ritual crafting and spells, but you may also have words to say after to empower and solidify your intentions and purposes.

Your words are specific to what you are celebrating and can be as simple or as elaborate as you choose. A sample of some words for a basic spell honoring the Triple Goddess on a Full moon ritual might be as follows:

Triple Goddess of the Moon, I honor thee with the power of three. *[light three candles, one for each aspect of the Goddess, as you speak the following lines]*

Maiden sweet of springtime moon, I light this candle to honor you. *[light the maiden candle]*

Mother full of the summer moon, I light this candle to honor you. [light the mother candle]

Crone in depth of darker moon, I light this candle to honor you. [light the crone candle]

Sacred Goddess throughout the year, on this full moon, I honor you here. [light your Triple Goddess herbs with fire to burn in your cauldron]

Bring to me your power of life, birth-death-rebirth, on full moon's light. [pour wine, water, or another beverage into your chalice]

I drink to thee, by the power of three, to honor your sacred wisdom. [take three sips from the chalice, one for each aspect of the Goddess, with the next three lines]

To the maiden [sip]

To the mother [sip]

To the crone [sip]

By this full moon, I honor your vision.

So, mote it be!

Wicca is a creative practice and poetry of magical intention. Your words can be designed by your power and so anything you choose will specifically empower your spells and rituals to help you access deeper wisdom and scared connection to the great divine.

Plan out what words you will say before your ritual and have them available to read if you do not know them by heart.

Step 8: Closing Your Circle

Once you have performed all of the steps included in your ritual, you begin to close the circle. Use the same steps you learned in

Chapter 4 about how to close your circle and let your intentions carry forward into your life after your closing practice.

You may choose to decorate your altar with any of your ritual ingredients and you will want to organize your tools back on your altar so they can be ready for the next ritual you are planning.

After the Ritual

After your ritual, having returned your tools and ingredients, and closed your circle, you can now work with the energies you have called upon to help you on your path of magic. Your altar serves as a reminder to you what rituals you have performed and why keeping your intentions alive and your focus pure.

The energy of your ritual will only last for so long, and so you will need to decide when to move forward, clearing your altar of any remaining components of your last ritual practice. You want to keep your energy flowing, as is with all-natural rhythms in life.

Use your intuition to know when the powerful energy of your ritual has waned and when it is time to send that ritual forward into the next plane of spirit. You will know the more your practice and tap into your inner guidance as you perform more magic throughout your practice.

Practice

The practice is potentially the most exciting part about Witchcraft and Wicca. The practice consists of thing a witch will obtain and then use it in their rituals or ceremonies.

There are spells for all kinds of purposes and solutions. Before every spell or ritual, the practice takes preparation and a sense of knowledge about the intent behind the magick. Throughout this book you have heard and read the words 'magic,' and 'magick,' but maybe never knew the difference or what the individual words mean.

Magic with a "c" defines a method of manipulation into the physical world through metaphysical means by applying ritual activity. Magick with a "k" is a much more defined sense.

According to Aleister Crowley, who founded the religion Thelema and associated with modern occultism used the word as a way to differentiate the two. Magick with a "k" is different than magic with a "c" because it separates stage magic from Wicca and ritual magick. Crowley's primary reason for adding a "k" to the end of the word is that considered magick to be anything a person is moved by, and fulfilling their true destiny, in which he called "true will."

Crowley put a lot of thought into the letter "k". Magic is a five-letter word, but he needed it to be six, as six represents the hexagram - a six-sided shape. "K" is the eleventh letter in the alphabet which also held importance to Crowley. Six-sided shapes and numbers or words were influential in his writings as well.

So, in other words, magic with a "c" is for magicians who use tricks with cards and create illusions in the regular person's eye as a way to wow them. Magic, with a "k" represents the magick that is used in Wicca and spiritual practices.

Wiccan Ritual Preparation

With magick comes ritualistic practice. Witches will gather ingredients, pull energy from the Earth, and then make wherever their designation for practice is, suited for the occasion. Most ritualistic preparation stems from the Gardnerian traditions of Wicca or is used as a basic outline and setup. Each witch does their thing, and each ritual is a little different but with many similarities to the following formula.

Purifying

The first thing witches will do to prepare for their ritual is to purify a circular area to rid bad energy or unwanted spirits. A witch will use a bristled broom to sweep the area, then burn sage above their head while walking along with the circular pattern. They will then pause at the north, east, south, and west sides of the circle. Every witch involved will burn sage and whisk it around their body.

Setting up the altar

On the east side of the circle, an altar is set with candles to represent the Gods and Goddesses. Also, on the east side, salt and water are set d for purification, then the athames of High Priest and Priestess, and finally incense. In each of the other four areas - north, south, and west - candles are lit and placed gently.

Casting the sacred circle

The highest members of the coven (or yourself) called the High Priest and Priestess will then cast the Sacred Circle. The circle is thought to be a spot that is without place or time and is cast by marking the edges with an athame or another tool, such as a sword, staff, or wand. They purify circle once more with salt and water, by placing three pinches of salt into the water and stir it specifically nine times with the athame.

The mixture is then sprinkled around the perimeter of the circle. Finally, incense is lit and carried around the circle.

Calling the quarters

Every witch (or just yourself) will then chant together calling the spirits of the four elements - Earth, fire, water, and air. These elemental spirits are guidance and protection for the witches.

Invoking the deity

A deity is needed for the witches to be able to perform magick, so the last step is to call upon them. Depending on the ritual, it can be a god, goddess, or both together. They are called by chanting out their names or reciting the gods and goddesses related to the ritual being done.

After this preparation is completed for the ritual, the witches will then begin whatever they were planning to perform. Once the ritual is finished, the ritual must end, which involves closing the circle.

To close the circle, you will do the same thing you did when you prepared for your ritual, only backward. The deities are thanked for their guidance and protection, the quarters are released, and the High Priests and Priestesses 'take d' the circle. They do this by walking around the perimeter of the circle, opposite of the direction they started, with the athame pointed outward - away from them. Once the Circle is d, the witches help gather up the supplies and go about their days as normal.

The Tools Used in Rituals

Not all religions or rituals need 'tools' but most rituals do require them. In the Neopagan religion, various magick tools were used in their practice. Each tool has its purpose and serves as direct magical energy. They are each usually established at an altar inside a Sacred Circle. In many Pagan traditions and Witchcraft, the witches will consecrate their tools before they use them.

To consecrate means to bless the items, they do this to purify them before they interact with the Divine, and also to rid the items of any negative energy that may be attached to them. In most cases, consecrating an item is a sure way to rid the tool of its history, so it is fresh and new with positive energy before you use it.

In other religions, the witches feel as though there is no need for consecration because whatever energy they are putting forth is already going into their tools, so consecrating them would only disrupt their energy flow. The bottom line, though, is that the choice is yours. There is a simple ritual in how to consecrate your tools, you can do this with jewelry, clothing, or the altar.

You consecrate it by offering the tool to the powers and energy of the four elements in which the tool becomes blessed in all directions. Many religions follow the same guidelines, but also have their ways of doing things for more experienced witches.

In the consecration ritual, you will need these ingredients, with each pointing in a certain direction.

- A white candle - Pointing south for fire
- A cup of water - Pointing west for water
- A tiny bowl of salt - Pointing north for Earth
- An incense - Pointing east for air

If your ritual consists of you making a Sacred Circle, it is best to do this now. Light the candle on the south side, and burn incense on the east side. Then, take the tool you are using or going to use, and hold it over the salt to the north and say:

"Powers of the North,

Guardians of the Earth,

I consecrate this wand of willow (or knife of steel, amulet of crystal, etc.)

and charge it with your energies.

I purify it this night and make this tool sacred."

After this, turn to the East and hold the item over the incense and say:

"Powers of the East,

Guardians of the Air,

I consecrate this wand of willow

and charge it with your energies.

I purify it this night and make this tool sacred."

Next, it's time to face the South, holding the tool over the flame of the candle, being careful not to burn it. And say;

"Powers of the South,

Guardians of Fire,

I consecrate this wand of willow

and charge it with your energies.

I purify it this night and make this tool sacred."

Finally, turn to the West, and pass your tool over a cup of water and repeat:

"Powers of the West,

Guardians of Water,

I consecrate this wand of willow [or knife of steel, amulet of crystal, etc.]

and charge it with your energies.

I purify it this night and make this tool sacred."

Return to your altar, point the athame to the sky, and repeat:

"I charge this wand in the name of Old Ones,

the Ancients, the Sun and the Moon and the Stars.

By the powers of the Earth, of Air, of Fire and Water

I banish the energies of any previous ers,

and make it new and fresh.

I consecrate this wand, and it is mine."

Once you have done this with every tool that you intend to use, the ritual is complete. Not only have you blessed your tool or item for future rituals, but you have also claimed this item as yours.

When you do this, you are strengthening the energy inside the tool, and binding your strength with it. The great part about consecration is that if you have consecrated your main tool - a wand, athame, chalice, amulet, etc... you can use that to consecrate any item you need to in the future.

The question you may be wondering now is, what exactly are the tools used in rituals. It depends on what ritual you are practicing, and it also depends on the witches' preference.

However, for the most part, fourteen different tools can be used in any ritual. When first starting as a practicing witch or Wiccan, you may have the urge to go d to your nearest "witchy" shop and buy everything that you may think you will need.

The books you have read, and the study guides you have purchased all tell you that you need gems, crystals, wands, etc... the list goes on.

Although it is good to be prepared, every tool has its specific purpose and needs to be used appropriately. The following list should give you a sense of what you will need, and what you don't.

Every religion Pagans, Wiccans, or others have their tools and use all of them differently, so it is up to you to explore and figure out what you need most.

The Altar

The altar is usually found in the center of a Pagan ritual and is a table used to hold the tools you are about to use for your ritual. You can choose to keep it up year-round or have a seasonal altar that changes as the Wheel of the Year turns. Some witches have more than one altar in their home normally represent their ancestors. The ancestor altar holds things like photos, ashes, heirlooms, and passed d journals or books.

Other themed altars include nature or Earth altars which hold unusual rocks, or crystals, pretty seashells, and sand from different parts of the world.

The nature altar may have chunks of wood or patterned flowers and wreaths for different seasons. The main purpose of an altar is to have your most valued items on there that suit the needs and purpose of you and your Witchcraft.

Athame

An athame is a tool many Wiccans and Pagans use for directing energy in their rituals and is often used for casting the Sacred Circle. The athame is generally a double-edged sword or dagger and is never used for actual cutting.

A bell

It is believed that loud noise drives evil spirits or demons away, which is what the bell is used for in most cases. The vibrations from the bell represent harmony as it includes, the shaking of a sistrum, a rattle, or the sound of a "singing bowl." In some religions or practices, the bell is used to start or end a rite, and to call a Goddess.

Besom

The besom is a straw broom and is used for sweeping a ceremonial or ritualistic area. Sweeping clears out any negative energy that may exist in the given space. The broom signifies as a purifier so it is linked to the water element.

Book of Shadows

A book of shadows is a Wiccan's or Pagan's memory or grimoire loaded with information. It generally contains spells, rituals, charts, the Theban alphabet, and the many rules of magick, plus much more. A Book of Shadows is a personal thing and should contain information that is most valuable and beneficial to you.

Candles

Candles hold many purposes and come in many colors. Besides just holding the element value of fire, and to call upon Gods and Goddesses, they are used in many spells. The idea behind the flame of the candle is that it obtains and holds your energy, while at the same time gets released into the atmosphere as it burns. In some religions, candles are thought to be more powerful if you make them yourself.

The Cauldron

The cauldron represents that of a chalice and is mainly feminine as it holds a womblike structure. The various ways you can use your cauldron for are:

- Burn incense, candles, or other offerings to the Gods inside it
- Use it with nothing inside to represent the Goddess of your ritual
- Blend herbs and other natural things for magical workings
- Fill it with water for moonlight scrying purposes

Cauldrons are not suitable for food if you are using them for magical rituals. If you are going to use a cauldron for food, make sure you have a separate one specifically for this purpose.

Chalice

Much like the cauldron, the chalice is also another feminine tool as it also holds the shape of a womb. It represents the water element and is used as a parallel tool to the athame in some religions.

This is so that together, the tools can represent the female aspect of the Divine during a token of re-enactment for the Great Rite. There are different kinds of chalices and are often silver or pewter but all mainly act as the same thing. Some rituals have water put in the chalice and it gets passed around to other members of a coven during a ritual to bond or tie the witches together.

Crystals

Upon thousands of stones or 'crystals' that are out there, the purpose or intent behind your practice solely depends on you and which crystal to use for this purpose. We will talk more about crystal properties later in this chapter, but when using a crystal, it is best to pick one based on their attributes. Birthstones also work great for the practice of magical workings and spells. Before using a crystal, it is best to cleanse it or consecrate it.

Pentacle

Most traditions and religions use the pentacle - not to be misunderstood by the pentagram - the pentacle is a flat piece of wood, metal, clay, or wax that has magical symbols engraved in it. The most common symbol is the pentagram which is a five-pointed star. This is why the two terms are confused or mislead but they are much different. The pentacle is often used for protection, but in some Wiccan practices, it is seen as an element of Earth.

Robe

The robe is a piece of clothing, that when put on is a preparation for the ritual to begin. In some covens, you may have a certain color of the robe that you would have to wear. The color represents the level of witch you are or how powerful you are - just like the belts in taekwondo. The robe also presents your mind with a sense of stepping from the mundane world to the spiritual and magical one that you are practicing.

The Staff

The staff is not always needed, but many Wiccans and Pagans opt for the staff as it is associated with power and authority. In some coven or traditions, only the High Priest and Priestess are allowed to have one. The staff is considered male energy and represents the Air element

Wand

The wand is one of the most popular magical tools used in every tradition or ritual. The wand is used for directing energy and represents male energy, power, and masculinity. It uses the Air or Fire elements and can also be used to consecrate items or call a deity. The traditional wand is made from wood, but others are made from glass, copper, silver, and other metals. Witches that do not use athames would instead use a wand for their rituals and practice.

A lot of these items you can make yourself; however, each tool has its special skill and ability for the purpose you are using it for.

Music and Magic

Music is used in Witchcraft or Wiccan practice because it helps call on spirits and Gods or guides to help with the ritual. Music is the language of spirit, and oftentimes in the religion, the instruments will be made from scratch with that of nature.

The natural sounds implemented in Wiccan practice is to raise powerful energy, alter consciousness, and connect you to deities.

Old day Wiccans created their instruments as a way to connect to Earth and nature. They would carve out the middle of a log to make a drum, found rocks that rang when hit, and flutes were made from bones and shells.

The main purpose of these instruments was to create sounds of nature such as the whistling of birds, the windy breeze, drumming of the rain, etc.

There has always been a hidden and deeper meaning behind the music that words can never explain. Music connects us to our internal selves and it gives voice to our dreams and desires. As music can help us connect deeper to ourselves, it also helps deities and powerful energies connect with us as well.

Instruments considered during your practice are:

Drums

The drum helps us stay grounded or connected when we are practicing a difficult spell or ritual. It is the representation of Gaia's heartbeat so the repetition of the drum helps us stay focused and come back to Earth if we need it. The drum is also useful for when we need to call upon the guidance or nurture from the goddess.

The Flute

The flute is a wind instrument that is directly associated with the Air element. Since the Air element represents intellect, these types of instruments are used to increase the witch's psychic abilities, improve knowledge, and find or possess wisdom. The Flute is used to call upon the god.

The Guitar

The guitar is a fire element and is used in spells and rites of sexuality, health, strength, passion, change, courage, and to get rid of bad habits. They are also used for purifying purposes so they will be strung or played before a ritual. The guitar helps to call upon the gods.

Resonant Metals

Resonant metals are things like gongs, cymbals, and bells. They associate with the most psychic of the elements, Water. Water represents healing, fertility, psychic power, friendship, love, and happiness due to its purification properties. The resonant metal instrument is mainly used to call the Goddess and is solely connected to nature.

These instruments are just a few tools that can be used before and during a ritual. Each instrument has its unique attributes to produce its power and that of a witch.

Spells

Wiccan spells are spell castings that are done by a Wiccan witch. Not all Wiccans practice magick, but the ones that do usually use the Book of Shadows for their guide. Spellcasting is about collecting your internal energy and power to direct it toward some sort of change in the world. Much like a ritual, spell casting can be done in different ways. Witches will draw energy from visualizing it, lighting candles, making herbal or crystal work, or by 'magical power' around them.

Any one person can cast a spell, but if you want it to work, it takes knowledge, practice, and concentration. You use your concentration on what your intentions are, become sensitive to your internal energy and the energy around you, and communicate with your 'Higher Self.' If you have not succeeded in doing so, then your spell may not work.

When casting spells, you need to understand the 'rules' of Witchcraft. These rules are set in place to protect you from accidental consequences and bad things returning to you. Consider reaching out to an experienced individual to help you, and guide you.

There are different types of spells like love spells, binding spells, and protection spells, for example. You wouldn't want to force someone to fall in love with you, so instead, you would use the love spell to have them shine more brightly than normal.

Because Wicca is about positivity, you always want to use the spell casting you are doing for good, not bad as you will want to be careful about the "Law of Threefold Return". So, if you intend to use a binding spell to get someone away from you, instead you would use a protection spell that will come in use.

When starting with spellcasting, it is so important to talk to someone experienced so that protection spells or whatever you try to do will work, and not fail unintentionally.

There are many protection spells however, most of them follow this formula:

You will need:

- A photo of yourself
- Four blue candles, or one white
- Essential oil for your astrological sign
- Sage for purification
- Three acacia leaves
- Three black tourmaline stones

The Spell:

- Wash your hands in a bowl of your essential oil and water, salt water will work also.
- Prepare your Sacred Circle by placing a blue candle at the East, South, West, and North regions of your circle.
- Place the white candle in front of you
- To the left of the white candle, is where the incense is placed. To the right, would be the tourmaline stones.
- Place your photo in front of the candle
- Cast your circle and light the incense
- Pass your photo over the incense three times and imagine you being surrounded with purity
- Hold in your hands, the acacia leaves, and the black.
- Visualize yourself surrounded in a bubble of white light. Send your love, healing protection energies straight into this light to make the protection full.
- To end the ritual or spell, ground your energy, blow out the candles, and close the circle. Keep the incense burning until it is finished.

Spells can create positive change for you. Wiccan spells are to never harm you or someone else, and it can also protect you and the ones you love from harm. If the spells do not work, then you need more practice and are not experienced enough. Understand in-depth about the Law of Threefold before casting any spell.

Also, when doing Wiccan spells, you need to understand that none of it is dark, so it may not be as powerful as "black magick" but it's better than having darkness take over you.

Colors and Crystals

Colors mean many things and can boost your energy and power. Below is a table of the meanings of colors in Wiccan traditions. If any color holds a different meaning to you, then use your intuition and substitute when practicing.

Color	Attributes	What they are used for
Red	Love, bravery, strength, deep emotions	Love, physical energy, health, psychic ability
Orange	Energy, allure, vitality, arousal	flexibility to changes, motivation, power
Yellow	Knowledge, inspiration, creativity	Communication, trust, fortune-telling, study
Green	abundance, growth, riches, rebirth, balance	Prosperity, Careers, fertility, wellness
Blue	Serenity, truth, knowledge, protection, tolerance	Healing, psychic ability, peace in the home, sympathy
Purple/violet	Spirituality, knowledge, dedication, harmony, idealism	Prophecy, Enhancement of nurture abilities, balancing sensitivity
White	Peace, purity, enlightenment	Cleansing, clarity, spiritual growth, and tolerance
Black	Protection, stability, respect	Ridding negativity, reformation
Silver	Wisdom, intellect, memory	Spiritual development, ridding negativity, mediation
Gold	Internal strength, self-realization, understanding, instinctual increase	Success, commitment, wealth, divination
Br	Endurance, stability, grounding, durability	Balance, focus, companion animals
Grey	Stability, neutrality, reflection	Making decisions, binding negative influences, reaching an agreement
Indigo	Emotion, insight, fluency, gracefulness	Meditation, spiritual healing, transparency of purpose
Pink	Affection, friendship, companionship	Romance, Spiritual awakening, relationships, children's magick

There are hundreds of gemstones and crystals out there to choose from. The table below consists of the most known crystals and their magical purposes in Witchcraft and Wiccan/Pagan belief.

Each crystal serves its purpose, and so when doing a ritual or a spell, make sure you choose one that works with you - not against you.

Gemstone	Properties
Amethyst	Stands for self-discipline, pride, sobriety, internal strength, peace, and self-awareness. Used for calming fears, and promote harmonious dreams and hopes. It heightens psychic abilities, increases one's true touch with themselves. It can be worn during meditation.
Tourmaline	Promotes emotional stability, break bad habits and urges, end negativity, and cleanses one's aura. It provides structure and prevents negativity from entering one's life. It is believed to calm the mind and body representing joy and protection internally and externally.
Citrine	Attracts warmth, happiness, and sun energies. Promotes friendship, communication, and independence.
Lapis Lazuli	Promotes truth, inner power, insight, openness, and spiritual growth. Increases intuition and helps you listen for your soul calling to guide you on your spiritual path helping you become more aware.
Moonstone	Associated with the moon, intuition and instinct, life cycles, balance, empathy, and clairvoyance. It is believed to bring someone to a deeper understanding of their feelings and what is in their heart when worn.
Quartz Crystal	This stone is worn for balance, cleansing, healing, personal power, and energy. It promotes spiritual growth and enlightenment
Rose Quartz	Promotes love, happiness, harmony, forgiveness, and understanding. Someone would wear rose quartz to boost self-confidence and reveal their inner beauty. It attracts friendships, relationships, romance, and close bonding interpersonal relationships.
Serpentine	Attracts love, luck, longevity, joy, serenity or peace, knowledge, and generosity.
Tiger's eye	Represents truth, integrity, honor, loyalty, willpower, and courage. It is associated with luck and protection. It helps someone decrease illusions, aid perceptiveness, and reveal truths. It also helps people become aware of other dishonesty and true intentions.
Turquoise	Promotes happiness, inner beauty, harmony, relaxation, and contentment. It's associated with love, prosperity, friendship, and protection. Turquoise is a stone that once worn, attunes its ability to the person wearing and increases its power focusing on where the person most needs it.

There are plenty more gemstones, each with their individual uses, which would take up an entire book. However, the crystals provided above should get you started on your path to finding what works best for you.

Herbs, Plants, and Essential Oils

Witches will use herbs, plants, and essential oils for their traditional ritual practice and spell castings. Each her, plant, or essential oil has their focus, and it is up to the individual witch on which to choose for their practice or ritual.

An herb is not a tree or a shrub, and so the term 'herb' from a witch's purpose is to define them as a plant that is useful without its regard to its lifestyle. Herbs in this sense do not include fruit, vegetables, or food purposes. The table below represents the main herbs that a witch will use in their practice.

Herbs	Magical Purposes	Uses
Cinnamon	Spiritual quests, augmenting power, love, success, healing, cleansing.	Digestive aide in tea form. Balances the gut after heavy a heavy meal or dessert. Makes a good anointing oil for a magical purpose.
Clove	Dispels negativity and bind people who speak bad of you, worn as a protective charm. Cleansing and purification	Used as an antiseptic for tooth pain and deterrent for colds; eases nausea and vomiting, and prevents disease and illness or infection
Coriander	Protecting the home, used in ritual drinks. Burnt on incenses for life longevity and love spells.	Makes a good love potion for two consenting parties. Also used in love sachets and charms.
Rose	Love, friendship, luck, protection, psychic power, and divination	Rose petals are used in honey to ease nausea and sore throats. They are high in Vitamin C
Rosemary	Improves memory, sleep, purification, youth, love, power, healing, protection, and wisdom	It is an antiseptic to wounds and can be a stimulant. Treats cases of flu reduce stress and headache or pains. Mental and

		physical boosters. Many benefits to rosemary.
Thyme	Sleep, psychic ability, courage, healing, purification, incense magical cleansing. and warding off negative spirits and energy.	Antibacterial, antibiotic, and diuretic properties. Treats whooping cough, warts, rheumatism, and acne. Very good for other things such as colds, touches of flu, fevers, etc.
Pine	Attunement to nature, balance, cleansing, healing, focus, purification, fertility.	Add to bathwater to ease aches and pains or swelling. Suited for its aromatic qualities bringing balance, and enhancement to nature.
Aloe	Beauty, protection, success, peace, and harmony.	Treats wounds and maintains healthy skin. It is applied in gel form for burns and relieves rashes. It helps to combat infections and growing bacteria.
Angelica	Protection	Grow in the garden as a protection aid. Carry the root with you for protection also.
Anise	Protection, purification, awareness, and happiness	Treats coughs, bronchitis, and stuffy noses. Prevents bad dreams, relieves an upset stomach, may help with menopausal symptoms.

Here is a table of essential oils that Wiccans will use in their Witchcraft:

Essential Oil	Metaphysical Properties
Bergamot	Increases money flow into your life, and magickal energy
Carnation	Increases physical and magickal energy, and is used in magick containing health and love.
Citronella	Clear your mind of negative energies and energizes your thoughts. Protects your Sacred Circle.
Cedarwood	Promotes spirituality and deepens your link to the deity. Involves self-control
Dragon's Blood	Purification, ritual magick, love, protection, and exorcism
Eucalyptus	Heal a room or house of negative psychic energy.
Frankincense	Heightens your awareness of spiritual realms, deepens the religious experience, reduces stress, and promotes higher consciousness.

Lavender	It involves health, love, and harmony. It decreases depression and anxious feelings and also helps with sleep and relaxation.
Peppermint	Self-purification and visualization.
Vanilla	Revitalizes the body, and can be used to channel into physical exertion or magick rituals. Inhale it to promote a loving sexual relationship.

Reality Manifestation

Reality is something that is a shared dream being manifested by everyone who shares it. It is linear time which means that we start at one end of the spectrum and move to the next in which the future is an illusion.

For example, think of a river; time is not consistent, but instead, it's our consciousness that moves through numerous timelines and experiences.

Every physical thing or possibility has already manifested or exists within a static hologram. It's like the mystical Kabbalah tree, which we will use to understand reality.

The branches represent our paths, which allow us the possibilities of our experiences, in which we can choose to take to learn from our life lessons. So, like "the law of attraction" what we put out into the world will eventually come back to us.

So, if we are giving out negative energy than we will attract negativity. Whereas if we adopt a positive mindset, what we attract is positivity.

The Manifestation Limits

Eventually, it may be possible to fly, or move mountains; however, some limits limit us from doing as we want. These limits are in place for safeguards to make us understand that what can seem like an impossible task will feel more attainable. Here are the limits:

Illusory limits

These limits exist in our minds and are our insecurities and false beliefs upon your intellectual and physical capabilities. For example, if you don't believe you can pick up a car to save a life, you will not physically be able to.

Practical limits

These limits are the things you cannot do YET, such as telepathy or moving objects with your mind. Overcoming the practical limits requires you to spiritually evolve to a place where you can do these things. This can be done through knowledge and awareness.

Imposed limits

This is a limit where a higher spiritual evolved being has placed on you. This could include your higher self or your high spiritual guides. First, you must learn the necessary lessons to overcome these barriers.

Implementing a positive mindset can be the thing stopping you from overcoming the limit you are faced with. A positive mindset is not just about keeping positivity in our lives, it's also about learning how not to push away the warning signs that a lesson is trying to teach us.

There are techniques to enable our reality creation. The following is just one example:

- Present yourself with the given moment. This will anchor you with what's happening right now. Once stabilized and grounded, picture a golden flame in the center of your heart. Then imagine the light of the golden flame escalating through your body.
- Now visualize the desired reality in as much detail as you can.
- The next step is to request or partition to all higher positive aspects of your consciousness and spirit.

If you are ready and at a place where your request can be answered, your reality that you envision will come true.

This is because our desired reality aligns with our actual reality and becomes synchronized. So, we cannot just wish for something and then have it happened right away. It takes practice and patience.

Remember, what you put out into the universe should repay you threefold. This is the law of attraction.

The Theban Alphabet

The Theban alphabet is also known as the Witch's Alphabet. It is a writing system with uncertain origins that came to publication in the sixteenth century. Another name for the Theban alphabet is "The Runes of Honorius". For the letters "j" and "u", the Theban letters are the same, and the same is true for letters "i" and "v".

This alphabet is used by witches to write their spells, inscriptions, and other important texts. People who do not know the Theban alphabet will not understand how to read it, and so it serves as a disguise to the blind eye. It also gives texts a mystical quality.

Conclusion

Did you get all your questions answered?

Which witch are you?

Which religion do you want to follow?

The purpose of this Wicca book for beginners is to help you understand Wicca and what it means to be a Wiccan. There are many benefits to practicing or joining Wicca, but unlike most religions, Wicca does not recruit members.

The purpose of this book is not to persuade you to join Wicca or dabble in Witchcraft; it simply will provide you with information and, in the end, you can do with it what you will.

One of the greatest benefits of Wiccan traditions is that the choice is always yours. You can choose what you want to participate in, which gods and goddesses to call upon, and what holidays you want to celebrate.

Dora McGregor

© Copyright 2019 Dora McGregor

All rights reserved

page intentionally left blank

WICCAN SPELLS

A Book of Shadows for Wiccans, Witches and Practitioners with Candle, Crystal, Herbal Healing, Protection Spells for Beginners

Dora McGregor

© Copyright 2019 Dora McGregor

All rights reserved

Wiccan Spells

© Copyright 2019 Dora McGregor All rights reserved.

Written by Dora McGregor

First Edition

Copyrights Notice

No part of this book may be reproduced in any form or by any electronic or mechanical means, including information storage and retrieval systems, without written permission from the author.

Recording of this publication is strictly prohibited and any storage of this document is not allowed unless with written permission from the publisher.

All rights reserved. Respective authors all copyrights not held by the publisher.

Pictures inside this book are of the respective ers, granted to the Author in a Royalty-Free license.

All trademarks, service marks, product names, and the characteristics of any names mentioned in this book are considered the property of their respective ers and are used only for reference. No endorsement is implied when we use one of these terms.

Limited Liability

Please note that the content of this book is based on personal experience and various information sources, and it is only for personal use.

Please note the information contained within this document is for educational and entertainment purposes only and no warranties of any kind are declared or implied.

Readers acknowledge that the author is not engaging in the rendering of legal, financial, or professional advice. Please consult a licensed professional before attempting any techniques outlined in this book.

Nothing in this book is intended to replace common sense or legal accounting, or professional advice and is meant only to inform.

Your particular circumstances may not be suited to the example illustrated in this book; in fact, they likely will not be.

You should use the information in this book at your risk. The reader is responsible for his or her actions.

The information provided herein is stated to be truthful and consistent, in that any liability, in terms of inattention or otherwise, by any usage or abuse of any policies, processes, or directions contained within is the solitary and utter responsibility of the recipient reader.

By reading this book, the reader agrees that under no circumstances is the author responsible for any losses, direct or indirect, which are incurred as a result of the use of the information contained within this document, including, but not limited to, errors, omissions, or inaccuracies.

Table of Contents

Introduction

A spell is any kind of experience that includes the intention to manifest something into your physical life experience. A spell is a direct line of communication between you and the cosmos to achieve a goal. A spell is your voice and action asking for what you want to occur and giving energy to the outcomes through creative expression.

Spells come in a variety of shapes, sizes, formats, colors, aromas, and they occur at different dates, times, moons, seasons, and so on. There are limitless possibilities when working with magic and manifestation, and that is all it is: a way to show yourself and the energy of all life, who you are, and what you want.

A spell can be anything that you want it to be and is ultimately a creative process to give you insight and support in where you want to go in your practice. Once you get the hang of using a few simple spells from this book, you will gain the confidence to start creating and utilizing your spells. With any spell, you will always work with specific intentions and find the best methods that will work for you along the way.

What you may be thinking, at this point, is how does a spell work? As you have read, a spell is a tool of manifestation. It is a powerful way to take the time to set a focused goal or intention through the use of specific ingredients, timing, and clarity of thought.

Spells are a way for you to gain an energetic connection to the reality you are working to create and set into motion. For a lot of Wiccans who practice magic, spells are the gateway to link with spirits and the great divine. You can easily transport yourself into another realm when you are in a circle cast for protection, imbuing the space with your precise intentions and magic ritual. It is a sacred dance that calls upon the energies of all that is around you to hear your call for something relevant to your life.

A spell works as an opening and affirmation of what energy you want to promote, enhance, and delegate to the earthly plane of reality. It is the energy that you hone and connects to so that it can be powerfully, elegantly, and eloquently delivered into the energy of everything around you. It is a ripple effect made possible by the stones you cast into the waters of life. It's not just as simple as an affirmation that you repeat to yourself over and over, although words are heavily used in casting spells. So much of asking for what you want from the Universe includes a special time, space, ritual, ingredients, and connection to your deities and honoring of the elements, at least from the Wiccan point of view.

Wiccan spells are a creative life force waiting for you to breathe them into existence. Your spells will hold the key to aligning with your powerful, personal magic and will help you work more closely with the Wiccan beliefs of harmony, balance, and nature. Wiccan spells will introduce you to working with some or all of the following manifestation practices:

- Candle magic
- Herbal magic and remedy
- Honoring Gods, Goddesses, and Deities
- Moon cycle power
- Crystal magic
- Elemental magic
- Creative visualization
- Altar space and consecrated or charged tools for your work
- Sun cycles
- Seasonal celebrations
- Harvest
- Empowerment, wealth, prosperity, protection, love, abundance, good luck, and good health
- Spiritual awakening and communication with the divine

- And more!

Wiccan spells are a gateway to trusting your intuition, calling upon the universal energies, and celebrating nature and the Goddess and God. It is performing a ritual of manifestation using all that is around you and choosing the path that is right for you through your relationship with Wicca.

Grounding and Centering for Spell Casting

Success with spell casting isn't just about safety and what tools you might use; it's also about how you prepare your mind, body, and spirit. The idea behind grounding and centering is that you ask yourself to unite with your authentic energy and power to call upon the work you want to do accurately.

Calming the mind, focusing on your intentions, and getting aligned for your magical purpose is a massive part of how to successfully cast. If your mind is wandering and thinking about what you are going to need from the grocery store, then you won't be focused on your power for manifestation. A lot of people will sometimes consider the centering process as something very akin to meditation.

In general, meditation is an all-encompassing term that essentially asks you to clear your mind and stay focused on the moment you are in. Meditation is another way to describe the centering process to help you ready your energy to make magic.

Grounding is another term to help you understand the quality of vibration—or energy—that allows you to stay within the power of Earth and her abundant fuel for magic. To ground yourself is to connect to the floor of everything, everywhere. You ground into the floor of your body and mind, and you also ground into the energy of whatever deities you are supporting.

Grounding helps us to siphon any excess energy into the ground and then pull the available power endlessly from the Earth through

148

us. It is a way to help the direction of your energy flow so that you feel supported, balanced, and prepared for whatever spell or ritual you are about to perform. In many ways, the grounding and centering process is what directs your intuition, instinct, and power into what you are working on. It is a focus of energy on all levels.

Not everyone will ground and center before casting, and if you were to compare results of spells from someone who does and someone who doesn't, you might be surprised to find that there is more return for those who are practicing their groundedness before and after casting a spell.

For many who practice Wicca, the grounding process can occur with the casting of the circle, as this activity has very stabilizing, opening, and centering qualities. Before any spell, if you want to have greater success with manifestation, it is crucial to prepare your energy to work with it according to your wishes and goals.

Some people will use a circle of protection while others might use a specific meditation, incantation, or poem. You can also use crystals and stones that are specifically for grounding, and using incense and smudging can have a very centering and grounding impact.

You will need to determine the right method for you, and if you want to have success with your spells, consider a grounding and centering ritual before you get started to make sure your energy is in the right alignment with your spell's purpose.

When looking for spells that work, you must keep in mind that before you do, you must do all your research about Witchcraft. It's like trying to play or read music without knowing how to or without having any experience. There are all types of spells to learn including, love spells, healing spells, protection spells, money spells, banishing spells, and divination spells. If a spell you have tried or will try doesn't work right away it can be for many reasons.

The Gods don't feel as though you are ready yet, you haven't done enough research, you don't understand Witchcraft entirely yet, or you have not done the things for spiritual growth before you started.

Witchcraft is not about shooting powers from our fingers, moving things with our minds, or believe we can fly, or even that we get whatever we want just because we uttered some mystical language. Much of Witchcraft is deeply connected to nature and science. Just because we don't see the spiritual realm or world doesn't mean we cannot practice seeing it, or that it isn't there.

The same goes for Witchcraft. When it comes to implementing spells consider the following when it comes to herbs, potions, incense, drumming, chanting candle, and runes.

Herbs: Witches or naturopathic doctors have used herbs for thousands of years to produce medicine or give us a mood-altering drug. Witches will use certain herbs for healing purposes and other spells.

Scents: Even though scents do not cure a person of the disease, they still have other purposes like making our moods better and increasing our memory strength. Have you ever caught a smell of someone passing by you, and you instantly started feeling sad, or happy due to the attachment of that scent. That's because we attach scent to our memories.

Sounds: Sounds also affect the mind. If you have put on relaxing music that works in calming you or listened to hyped music to get you excited, this is a prime example of how sounds affect you.

Colors: Just like colors can be stimulating to our brains, it can also do wonders when you are producing a spell. Red excites, blue usually calm, and orange can make you hungry, which is why so many fast-food restaurants use this color.

Chanting: Ever sat in on a speech, or watched a movie that you pulled quotes from because they 'moved' you? This is how chants work in a ceremony or ritual. They are powerful when you want to succeed at a specific spell. Have you ever had a mantra for when you get anxious or your mod heightened? Did it make you feel better? Now you can see how words and chants or mantras can greatly affect your mind.

Meditation: Meditation brings our awareness of where we center our bodies and minds. It's when we are in a relaxed state of consciousness that the things around us can be absorbed. Meditation also promotes spiritual growth and healing.

Spells work much like this next example: Say you need to pass a test. So, you burn an orange candle and meditate solely on that candle, bringing your whole focus on the orange candle. At the same time, you will want to burn rosemary, then start chanting positive affirmations. You may say things like "I got this," "I will do great." "I am smart." etc... The orange candle represents intellect and focus, meditating on the candle brings you to a relaxed state of mind, and the rosemary is there to stimulate focus. The chanting is just you retraining or reprogramming your brain to do well.

One thing that is steady throughout this process is that you whole-heartedly believe. The same goes for spells, you must put your sole focus on exactly what you believe, because as you believe you will obtain what you expect to happen.

To have a spell become successful, your energy has to be incomplete balance with the intent of your desired results. You must ask yourself before casting spells what you want out of it. Are you looking for love spells? Do you need protection from someone or something? Do you want to bless your home?

How to start

Steps to Writing Your Spells

1: Determine Your Goal, Intention, or Magical Purpose

Quite possibly the most important step in designing your spell, the goal or purpose is what will help you structure everything about your spell. What are you wanting to accomplish? Are you looking for love? Are you trying to draw more financial abundance or prosperity into your life? Are you wanting to honor a specific deity?

There are a lot of possibilities and they all require a specific intention. Be clear. Be direct. Keep it simple. Know what it is you are trying to magically manifest in a very honest and direct format so you can build and create your spell around that goal.

2: Determine What You Will Need to Achieve Your Intention

Spells need tools and ingredients, although some might need only a candle or a crystal. Whatever you are going to need, you will need to decide your list of ingredients for your recipe. Some of the ingredients will come from the following list and all of them should be goal-specific according to your intention for the spell:

- Colorful candles
- Incense
- Herbs
- Objects from Nature
- Crystals and/or stones
- Altar Tools
- Bowls, containers, mixing spoons (all consecrated for rituals)
- Special garments
- Indoor or Outdoor set up/ altar (spell specific)

You may find even more items that you will need than what is listed here and you can always add things to every spell that you create based on what kind of Wicca you are practicing and what kind of spell you are casting.

3: Determine the Timing

Every spell has a different energy that needs to guide it. Your spell may need to fall on a specific date, or even at a specific time of day. You may need the full sun, shining d on your spell, or you may need the darkness and energy of a New Moon.

Every spell has time to make it work, and that time could also be anytime. Some spells will be open to work whenever you are needing them to be performed and the results may be different for you, depending on your approach.

Many Wiccans will cast their spells following what moon, or seasonal cycle they are in, to help the power of the spell feel enhanced or to generate a greater manifestation possibility.

Whatever time you decide to work your spell is important to the nature of your original goal. Choose the timing based on your intentions. If you are trying to grow your money and security, you may want to cast your spell on a New Moon and watch your money grow as the Full Moon grows, too. You may need the energy of the dawn hours to bring a powerful focused day and work experience into fruition, as a fresh start from the morning sunlight.

All of your spells can be written in the Book of Shadows you are building and it is helpful to give yourself feedback on the most powerful times to perform each spell. You may need to play around with the timing for each spell if you are repeating them so that you can hone in on the timing that manifests the greatest return for you.

4: Decide on Your Words and Incantations

As you learned from the Step-by-Step Guide for Rituals in the last chapter, your words are important. They carry the meaning of your goal into the energy of the Universe to help make it manifest, so you want to make sure that you are clear in your wording and meaning.

Writing your spell is a big part of the process and should always be done beforehand and not after you have cast your circle. If you want your spell to work, you need to find the right words for your goal. The world of magic isn't sinister, but it can have a sense of humor as to how you receive your rewards and gifts from your spell work. 'Be careful what you wish for' is a popular saying, and in spell casting, that couldn't be truer.

Make sure you know what you are asking for before you set your intentions. It will likely come back to you.

5: Organize the Spell into a Workable Format

Once you have determined all of the elements from Steps 1-4, you are now ready to construct the spell. They are the puzzle pieces and now you have to put the puzzle together. This part can be the most fun as it is the design phase of your spell.

Here is where you get to be the architect and determine what happens first, next, and last. You will decide when to light the ritual candles you have chosen, and what words you will say alongside the sacred act of lighting them. You will decide exactly what method you will take to incorporate your herbs (burning, drinking as a tea, displaying at the altar, wrapping for drying purposes, etc.).

You will decide when to speak the words of manifestation in conjunction with each sacred and magical act.

Building the spell is part of the work you will incorporate into your Book of Shadows. It acts as a journal of your writing spells and your progress with them, so don't be afraid if you have to scribble things out and change some elements and factors. It is an ever-evolving work of art, just like every spell you create and every piece of magic you perform.

6: Use Your Spells

After you have created your spell, the best part is using it. You will want to make time and space and collect all of your ingredients to have fun with your work of magic art. Using your spells is the payoff and the reward and your goals and intentions are set into motion every time you use them.

The next section will offer some basic spells to give you a place to start and familiarize yourself with some basic spell examples.

Don't hesitate to borrow these spells and change them to your liking.

Things to Consider when Casting a Spell

Enjoying your spell work is easy, especially when you are taking the right precautions. Even when you aren't using any potentially dangerous tools or implements, it is still a good practice to go into your work with a mindset of feeling prepared, protected, and safe.

Having a standard protocol for your witchcraft and spell work will help you remain respectful of yourself and all the energies that you choose to incorporate into your process.

Safety with Tools. You will find that a lot of the tools in this book and many that you find online or in other books will have a list of things you will need to accomplish the spell. Some of these tools will include flame, candles dripping hot wax, smoke for smudging, blades for cutting and other sharp tools for specific acts of manifestation, and many more.

The tools that you use will help you harness the energy and manipulate in the way that is required to achieve the final goal and outcome of your spell. All tools are sacred to your practice and should be properly cared for. Safety with tools isn't just about safe handling, which you will want to make sure of; it can also be about safe energy.

Consider how often you will be using these tools and how much energy they will accumulate over time. Cleansing and purifying your tools is an easy and effective way for you to keep your tools in a higher state of vibration and clarity for use in spell work.

Sometimes, the energy of something can feel "off," and you aren't sure why. This can happen with your tools for Wiccan spell work, and a "funky-feeling" tool can cause you to fumble and could even cause some injury.

Safe handling of candles, matches, fire, blades, and smudging sticks is always highly recommended. Make sure you have the right dishes and containers to keep your candles standing upright and your smudge stick away from anything it could set fire.

You may also want to make sure your altar and ritual space is well-ventilated while you use smoke for purification.

Practicing proper tool safety is a must, even when it means clearing and purifying the energy of your tools and implements regularly, to prevent them from collecting unwanted energies that could mar your spells and incantations or them make difficult.

Fire Safety. Fire safety should go without saying, but it bears mention here. However, fire comes into your rituals and spell work; it must be respected for the energy that it carries. Fire is a power of creation and destruction and has always been here to give us life and sometimes take it away. The reality is, fire is dangerous, and it needs to be used wisely.

Many spells call for candle magic for the lighting of sacred smoke and for burning of intentions, messages written on paper, and herbs. The use of fire and burning things is a very holy and magical

158

practice and will give a great deal of power to any spell work you choose to do when performed safely.

When you are using fire in your spells, take necessary precautions:

- Use a sturdy candle holder for every candle.
- Keep your candles out of strong winds and away from things that can easily burst in flames.
- If you are letting your candles burn d, then you will need to monitor them or make sure they are in a safe container.
- Have a dish for your smudge sticks to lay them in while they burn out, as well as your incense.
- Use a cauldron or fire-safe bowl to burn your written words on paper, herbs, or other items. You may even want to do your burning outside during spells, depending on the space and ventilation.
- Keep flammable items away from anything burning until the flames are put out.

Fire is powerful, and so is the magic it adds to your spell. Use it wisely, and it will help you to manifest your goals and spells very effectively.

Harm None. As you have already read in Chapter 1, an essential aspect of the Wiccan philosophy is that you will cause no harm to another while you practice magic. This is a potent tool to help you stay safe from causing damage to yourself and others while you cast. The Threefold Law states that anything you do can return to you three times, meaning your energetic impact through rituals and spells will return to you three times over.

That is incredibly powerful energy to return to you, and if you are casting to bring more wealth and abundance into your life, that would be a good thing. However, if you are casting a spell to make someone fall out of love with another person to fall in love with you, that is harmful to not only one, but two people. It will come back to you at some point by the power of three, according to Wiccan beliefs.

However it returns to you, it will likely feel bad and unpleasant, and so for the safety of your feelings and those of another, it is best to state the Wiccan Rede of "harm none," before you cast any spell to make sure you are not going to bring any hurt to you or another.

This is a powerful way for you to engage with magic more positively and beneficially to the good of all.

Spiritual Safety. Preparing to cast a spell requires an opening to all of the energies and a connection with spirit. Becoming wide open as a channel of energy during your spells and incantations requires some protection on your part to make sure you only include positive and light vibrational energies into your spellcasting.

Sometimes, when we are doing our work, we forget that we can easily open to all different kinds of nature, both dark and light and that it will be necessary to consider protecting yourself from anything that might have a negative impact or effect on your energy or your spells.

All this means is that you set an intention of protection and invite-only positive energies into your circle and your spell work. Some might even call upon a specific deity to act as a guardian during their spells to help them stay focused and keep any unwanted energies at bay.

Another excellent method of creating spiritual protection is through the casting of a circle.

Your Personal Safety and Well-Being. Your safety and well-being can have a significant impact on your ability to cast magic well and safely. If you are overworked, overtired, ill, or unhappy, it may not be the best time for you to be doing any casting work. That energy will carry through in your spell and can have an impact on your manifestation.

If your spell involves helping you out of those states of mind or being, then make sure you are gentle and nurturing and that you are performing your spells at a moment of optimal health to achieve your goal.

Your personal safety is just as important as the concept of harming none. Make sure you are in the right mindset and emotional state to perform magic. Remember, what you cast can return to you threefold, so whatever your intentions are, make sure you are in a good head, heart, and body space to perform your spell work.

Grounding and Centering for Spell casting

Success with spell casting isn't just about safety and what tools you might use; it's also about how you prepare your mind, body, and spirit. The idea behind grounding and centering is that you ask yourself to unite with your authentic energy and power to call upon the work you want to do accurately.

Calming the mind, focusing on your intentions, and getting aligned for your magical purpose is a massive part of how to successfully cast. If your mind is wandering and thinking about what you are going to need from the grocery store, then you won't be focused on your power for manifestation. A lot of people will sometimes consider the centering process as something very akin to meditation.

In general, meditation is an all-encompassing term that essentially asks you to clear your mind and stay focused on the moment you are in. Meditation is another way to describe the centering process to help you ready your energy to make magic.

Grounding is another term to help you understand the quality of vibration—or energy—that allows you to stay within the power of Earth and her abundant fuel for magic. To ground yourself is to connect to the floor of everything, everywhere.

You ground into the floor of your body and mind, and you also ground into the energy of whatever deities you are supporting.

Grounding helps us to siphon any excess energy into the ground and then pull the available power endlessly from the Earth through us. It is a way to help the direction of your energy flow so that you feel supported, balanced, and prepared for whatever spell or ritual you are about to perform. In many ways, the grounding and centering process is what directs your intuition, instinct, and power into what you are working on. It is a focus of energy on all levels.

Not everyone will ground and center before casting, and if you were to compare results of spells from someone who does and someone who doesn't, you might be surprised to find that there is more return for those who are practicing their groundedness before and after casting a spell.

For many who practice Wicca, the grounding process can occur with the casting of the circle, as this activity has very stabilizing, opening, and centering qualities. Before any spell, if you want to have greater success with manifestation, it is crucial to prepare your energy to work with it according to your wishes and goals.

Some people will use a circle of protection while others might use a specific meditation, incantation, or poem. You can also use crystals and stones that are specifically for grounding, and using incense and smudging can have a very centering and grounding impact.

You will need to determine the right method for you, and if you want to have success with your spells, consider a grounding and centering ritual before you get started to make sure your energy is in the right alignment with your spell's purpose.

How to Cast a Circle and the Reason Behind it

Casting a Circle is one of the most common aspects of practicing with Wiccan spells and all kinds of Pagan rituals and witchcraft.

First, let's talk about why you want to cast a circle before you start a spell. Then, you can see exactly how it is done.

A circle in Wicca and witchcraft serves multiple purposes. It is specific energy to help you feel safe and protected, while it calls upon the elements, directions, and spirit to help you in your work.

Traditionally, the circle is your gateway to magic and will always keep you in alignment with the energy of nature. Here, within the circle, you will find the support you need to accomplish your goals from all directions of the Universe.

You should always cast a kind of circle, even if it completely simple, like spinning in a circle to acknowledge energy around you that will shield you from outside forces. A circle is an energetic bubble that holds your power and your magic inside.

It can be a way to keep you spiritually safe, only inviting in the energies you want to work with.

Many will use a candle, an object from nature, or an altar tool to mark each direction with one of the four primary elements. The fifth element, spirit or ether, is what is above you. In Wicca, it can pertain to the God/Goddess energy you call upon to worship in your work.

The purpose of your circle is to protect you and also to empower you while you cast. It is a connection to the divine and promotes the gateway and opening for manifestation while it holds you in the balance of all life.

Basic Circle Casting

Opening a Circle

Use creative visualization to help you picture your circle and the protective shield that will surround you and your work. You can see it like a glass orb, a tent, or a colorful light surrounding you.

The size of your circle depends on the amount of space you need to work your spell. Use a compass if you don't know what way is north.

1) From the north position, use your finger or some other kind of tool to point in front of you or to the floor in the north of the circle. You can say something like this:

    "As I open to the divine powers that be, I call upon the power of the North and the Earth element to protect and guide me. And so it is."

2) Now, move clockwise to the East and say something like this:

    "As I open to the divine powers that be, I call upon the power of the East and the Air element to protect and guide me. And so it is."

3) Continue clockwise to the South and say: "As I open to the divine powers that be, I call upon the power of the South and the Fire element to protect and guide me. And so it is."

4) Continue to the West position and say:

    "As I open to the divine powers that be, I call upon the power of the West and the Water element to protect and guide me. And so it is."

5) Return to the starting position of the North and hold both hands above you, either clasped together and your fingers are pointing up or using a tool of your choice. Then connect to the element of spirit and say:

"I call upon the energy of the Universe and [insert preferred deities or other energies of spirit] to aid me in my magic. And so it is."

You can change the format according to your preferences and add any other information that feels the most grounding, opening, and balancing for you. Use creative visualization to picture guardian and ancestors with you, or use crystals and gemstones to create the entire circle, laying them out on the floor around you. How you choose to cast your circle must be a regular part of your preparation for a successful spellcasting.

Book of Shadow

Book of Shadows is vital in Spell Casting

A Book of Shadows has a long history in the world of witchcraft, Pagan arts, and various other forms of religion and magical devotion. It is the essence of every practitioner's work and can be seen as the lifelong journal, diary, or recipe book of all of your spells, rituals, symbols, beliefs, and preferred magical explorations.

Your Book of Shadows always comes in handy and allows you to grow and expand with your quest for knowledge in the magical and Wiccan arts. Not every Wiccan or Witch's Book of Shadows will look the same or have the same content, and that is why it is necessary to give you some information about what it is, where it comes from, what goes inside of it, and various forms of magic that you may choose to illustrate and depict in your Book.

History of the Book of Shadows

The traditionally known Book of Shadows has often been called a Grimoire throughout history. In myths and legends of magic and sorcery, famous wizards were depicted as having their sacred Grimoire that is full of spells, potions, and magic, where Merlin from the Legend of King Arthur is one of the most notorious.

Several versions of Grimoire, or Book of Shadows, have been published since the dawn of popular culture's embrace of Neo-Pagan religions, especially with the advent of Wicca, which was officially founded in the mid-1950s by Gerald Gardner, who is thought to be the originator of the term "Book of Shadows."

For Gardener, his Book of Shadows was his diary of all of his Wiccan worship, craft, rituals, information about deities, and so forth. Over time, it was added to and became the sacred volume of knowledge for his coven, and over time, it was the most famous book of the Wiccan religion.

It has been published several times, and since Wicca's debut in the mid-twentieth century, several other versions have been published by various authors and practitioners of Wicca and other Pagan arts. You can most likely find a Grimoire or Book of Shadows at your local book shop.

From the ancient times of early witchcraft and the need to organize herbal magic and remedies to the development of the Wiccan practice by Gerald Gardener through his Book, your Book of Shadows comes from a long history of magical people who knew how to detail their mysteries in one sacred text.

Why You Need a Book of Shadows

Having your Book of Shadows is an essential step for anyone who wants to practice the magical arts. Your Book is your way to enforce your beliefs, rituals, manifestations, and experiences while you go through the journey of awakening to your power as a person.

Many people view it as a journal of magical discovery, as it is something you can add to every day to note your progress, add new spells, make changes or write new notes in the margins about spells you have already cast and their development, and so much more.

Your Book is how you can keep yourself focused and organized with all of the work you want to do through your Wiccan practice. It has a way of becoming like a friend to you. It will hold many of your secrets and truths while you discover more about making your spells come to life.

There are so many different ways that it can be utilized on your path, and as you get more acquainted with casting, you will find more and more things that you want to add to it. It has an invaluable set of information and is your ultimate resource. Many

Wiccans and Witches will adopt another coven or solitary practitioner's published Grimoire to get going and have some ideas of what to put inside.

For you to get going with your Book of Shadows, you only need a few things to get you started. You can use any kind of notebook you like or find something exceptional that you want to keep adding to. You can always cut out pages that you have written notes on and tape or glue them into your main book. It's a creative process. Have fun with it!

Table of Contents: What's Inside?

What goes in your book of Shadows is up to you and your practice. If you are looking to join a coven, your coven will have its Book that you will likely have to copy and learn from, so you won't be creating yours. For the solitary practitioner, you will have authority over what goes in your Book, and it will always be unique to your adventures with magic.

Here are some of the things you may find in a Book of Shadows:

Book Title and Date. When did you start your sacred text?

Book Blessing. Say a few words on the first page, like an inscription, to bless your book, and let it know how much it will always mean to you.

Index. Give a brief overview of sections, like a table of contents, if that is how you wish to organize your book.

Some of the sections listed in your index might include the following:

Magical Rules and Principles. What are your personal beliefs or the rules you choose to follow in your practice? What are your spiritual values on your path?

Goals and Intentions. What are your short-term and long-term goals in your practice? Write how you plan to succeed in your goals, what you would like to achieve, and how long you plan to give yourself.

Record of Dreams and Divinations. What messages are you receiving from the spirit or your higher self through your dreams and divination experiences? Use your intuition to record your introspections and interpretations.

Research and Study. Keep a record of what you are discovering and learning along your path that feels important to your practice. Examples might be astrology, specific Gods and Goddesses, tarot, crystals, and their meanings, etc.

Spells and Incantations. Keep a space with plenty of room to write and add new spells and incantations. You may review some of your spells, and add notes or ideas to improve each one based on your experiences with them.

Ceremonies and Rituals. It's important to create a space where you can plan and detail your special ceremonies, celebrations, and rituals, depending on what your practice is and what you want to celebrate. Keep notes about how it went, what worked well, and how you might change it for next time.

Herbal Potions and Remedies. These are personal recipes for brews, potions, and concoctions for healing and magical purposes.

You can include some, none, or all of these sections, and you can also come up with as many others as you want or need. Organizing your Book of Shadows is unique to you and your practice. See it as your creative devotion to your spiritual journey and allow it to unfold with you over time as you grow.

White, Black, and Red Magic

Some other types of information that might be included in your Book of Shadows are the kind of magic you are working with. There is a lot of controversy and debate over good and evil and white and black when it comes to magical arts. Some say that if it's black, it's evil, but that is simply not the way it works. There is also red magic, which, for some, is uncommonly heard of and is often misinterpreted and misunderstood.

This section will give you a brief knowledge about the different types of magic and what they can mean to your Book of Shadows.

White Magic

White magic has its connotations in being pure, virtuous, healing, whole, and beneficial. It has been historically considered a more appropriate form of magic to practice; there has been much persecution of another color of magic (see the next section) that gave white magic a better name.

According to historical context, white magic is seen as a healer's magic. Wise men and women who practiced magic for selfless reasons and the good of others, both physically and spiritually, were considered to be practitioners of the white magic.

Other sources have also sh that white magic is simply a part of the balance between light and dark and has its focus on the more masculine qualities of Wicca. For example, the harmony between opposing forces is one of the central beliefs of Wicca, and for those who choose to practice white magic only, or intentionally, they are guiding their source of power through the lighter energies and have a superior opening to work with that kind of magic.

If you have ever seen the popular yin-yang symbol, you will be familiar with the energetic balance between light and dark forces or the divine masculine and feminine energies in all things. White magic perceives reality through the lens of the white and the light and is associated with male energies, action, force, healing, wisdom, and manifestation for the good of all. You can also perceive white magic in the feminine form as the Maiden aspect of the Goddess who is all light and pure and comes to life at the time of year when the light is returning to the days and the dark period is coming to an end.

Depending on what you choose to practice, white magic can also be incorporated into your research of a particular deity or God/Goddess aspect. It all comes d to your faith, intuition, and beliefs and how you choose to enjoy the forces of white, or light, magic.

Black Magic

You've probably read all kinds of things online about how dark or black magic is evil, and practicing it means that you are supporting a dark art. According to the internet and other religious concepts, black magic is associated with the Devil, evil, hexes, curses, and so on and is a large part of what caused some people to be burned alive at the stakes in the centuries of witch trials and persecution.

Amazingly, this is a fear-based identification and always was, and black magic has nothing to do with "evil" or the Devil. In the last section, you began to see how white magic is part of a greater whole. In the concept and beliefs of Wicca, a great honoring and devotion to the balance of all energies in life is a benefit to embracing the world of the divine and the cycles and rhythms of nature.

Black magic is another side of "all that is" and can be regarded as the shadow realm or shadow side of your Wiccan practice. Unlike white magic, black magic embraces the less appealing forces of nature, like death and banishing, deeper emotions, and uncomfortable realities. It is an excellent source of power from the perspective of balance and is a requirement to understand Wicca in general, as well as all of the energy in all life.

Black magic can be viewed as the feminine counterpart to the balance of black and white. It is the yin of the yin-yang concept and embraces the night, the dark time of year, the Crone phase, the waters and emotions of all life, death and rebirth cycles, as well as many other forces. It is an authoritative source of energy to incorporate into any practice and should never be considered as evil. If you are in alignment with the Wiccan Rede "harm none," then you will know that whatever magic you perform must be pure of heart and intention. Therefore, black magic is used in Wicca as a balance to the light and the white and is seen as a part of a greater whole.

Black magic is about power, protection, banishing negative energies, reversing hexes, creating healthy boundaries, resilience, self-control, healing from loss and grief, inner strength, and death.

It is a connection to the Crone, as well as the part of the cycle that embraces a darker night or the night of the soul and can be common among practitioners who worship a Crone Goddess like Hecate. It can also be viewed as masculine energy, depending on your practices and what deities you call into your circle for guidance and support.

Red Magic

There are a couple of interpretations of Red Magic that we will go over in this section. One of the more commonly known versions of red magic in culture revolves around the Hoodoo or Voodoo, which are practices brought to America from West Africa.

These practices have a lot of similarities to other forms of magic ritual and spell and are also often related to some form of Bible scripture, as well as the use of potions, brews, and herbs, as with other spells. Also, there may be the use of more bodily fluids, such as saliva, urine, blood, semen, and menstrual blood.

Another form of Red Magic that you may have heard about from online sources is the concept of sex magic and that it is often referred to as red magic. Sex magic has nothing to do with sexuality, promiscuity, kink, or any kind of sexual expression involving arousal and the intention of spicing up your sex life.

Sex magic is a way to create and promote a more powerful manifestation. The energy of orgasm is incredibly powerful, and when you are casting a spell or performing a ritual, using the power of your sexual energies and the balance of your masculine and feminine divinity, you can encourage and create a more powerful manifestation.

In general, it is suggested that you practice this kind of red magic on your before you would consider including a magical partner. It isn't about sexual outcomes with another person; it is about casting magic into the Universe of all things and all energy through the use of orgasmic power.

Red magic, on both fronts (Hoodoo and Sex), has more to do with the visceral physicality of our natural power and has a sharp and distinct potency to ask for what it is you want to manifest. More research may be required to incorporate a journey through Red Magic into your Book of Shadows, and it will be well worth it to ask a lot of questions before delving into what that will look like for your practice.

Symbols, Signs, Runes, and Rituals

Within every Book of Shadows, there will be an assortment of magical symbols, signs, and runes that can be utilized through your spellcasting work and rituals to empower the energy of your spells.

There are a large number of these symbols, and many of them come from a variety of cultures and religious backgrounds.

The best way to discover the magic of each symbol, sign, or rune is to find them through your research and expression of your craft. There are a variety of sources to find these symbols, and they will all serve a unique purpose to your spell work. Examples of some symbols are:

The Triple Goddess — It's waxing crescent moon on the left, a full moon in the center, and a waning crescent moon on the left (sometimes, a pentagram in the center of the full moon). It identifies the three stages of the Triple Goddess (Maiden, Mother, and Crone).

The Horned God — It's a circular shape to mark a head with sideways crescent moon laying at the top of the circle on its side (sometimes a pentagram in the center of the circle). It represents the masculine aspect of God/Goddess.

Celtic Knot Symbols — several variations of Celtic knots (i.e., Celtic Cross knot, Triquetra, and Odin's Cross). They are representative of various concepts like protection and calling on the God/Goddess.

Pentagram/Pentacle — The pentagram is one of the most notable of Wiccan symbols. It's a five-pointed star that relates to the five elements and is a symbol of protection and ritual consecration. The pentacle is a disc that can have any of the above-mentioned symbols inscribed on it, most often the pentagram.

The Elements — There are symbols for each of the four elements and the fifth Spirit, which can be engraved on anything magical in your work. They are representative of Earth, Air, Fire, Water, and Ether.

Runes are a whole other set of symbols in the form of an alphabet and have their origins in ancient Pagan religions and practices. Carved onto a piece of wood, bone, or stone, runes have an ancient symbolic meaning ascribed to each one and are used for divination and guidance in your practice.

As with the other signs and symbols listed above, runes can be written, inscribed, or carved into your ritual and spell ingredients to represent specific intentions and manifestations. These symbols are very useful as individual signs and can also be read together in a group to form a more accurate and detailed story or divination within your spells.

With all of these symbols and signs, you will also need to incorporate these magical engravings into your rituals.

Your Book of Shadows will contain a variety of different ceremonies, most often things that you will repeat within a season, cycle, or time of year. The symbols you choose to include in your ritual ceremonies will depend on what you are celebrating, and you can inscribe the runes or signs into the instructions for your ritual.

All of your practices will be decorated by the Universal and spiritual message of each unique symbol or talisman of energy, and as you grow your Book of shadows, keep a separate section of these pictures and their meanings so that you can draw upon them for your spellcasting needs and magical uses.

They are here to empower and invoke and will give you the right information to use when you are performing any ritual or spell incantation.

With all the details you have learned in this chapter about your personal Book of Shadows, you can now begin to craft it with the spells outlined for you in the next section. There is a variety of basic starter spells to get you started. Get yourself a big notebook and get excited to begin writing your very Book today!

Magic Spells

Moon Magic Spells

Since the dawn of our human civilization, our lives have been governed by the power of the Sun and the moon. The moon has played such a vital and important role in myths, traditions, cultural practices and beliefs, and religious interpretations.

For hundreds of thousands of years, it has been a great source of light, especially when it is full. It's also a way to help people structure and measure time.

The moon is closely connected with a variety of Goddesses and Gods all over the world and in various cultures, and throughout magic and mythology, it has been a central theme of human concerns like love, fertility, passion, death, and rebirth, mystery, femininity, and afterlife matters.

Today, the moon has its same magic and power and will continue to influence people's minds, bodies, hearts, and spirits, whether or not they practice Wiccan or any other kind of moon worshipping religion or practice.

The power of the moon is considered watery, feminine, receptive, and of the Goddess. It can sometimes feel magnetic, making you feel "pulled" towards its energy. For some, it is physically powerful; for others, it may just feel like a heightened sense of awareness or perception.

Because of this connection to intuitive powers, psychic sense, and powerful magnetism to the great Goddess divine, the moon is a vital mode of perception and ritual practices in magic. When we intentionally connect with the power of the moon, we are engaging a live channel of harmony with the energy of the moon's cycles, the rhythms of nature, and the divine consciousness of all things.

The moon helps us manifest desired changes in our lives through the various cycles and the kind of energy emitted from the ever-turning moon. Lunar phases are beneficial in determining and interpreting when and how to use the moon for your spells.

Lunar Phases and When to Use Them in Spells. Witches and the moon are old hats. Witches have been dancing under moonlight since the birth of humanity, and so it goes without saying that if you are a practicing Wiccan or witch, you will find yourself in some connection or devotion to the moon and her vital energies and cycles.

Some will say that the moon is the most potent energetic force to affect your magic spells, rituals, and incantations. There are a variety of reasons people may think this way: the moon affects the tides, menstrual cycles, moods, and so forth. That is some pretty powerful pull to have such an impact as that. The entire ocean ebbs and flows because of the moon. Think about that for five minutes.

Some Wiccans and witches will not bother as much with magical timing, and everyone will see fit to develop their unique and individual practices and techniques along the way. You may have to do some experiments to determine what is best for you. If you are interested in using the potent magic of the moon for your spells and craft, you will likely notice the impact of that magic overall on any of your spellcraft. See a quick overview of the moon phases below.

Phases of the Moon

Phase: Dark Moon

Appearance: Invisible

Approx. Rising Time: Sunrise

Approx. Setting Time: Sunset

Phase: Waxing Crescent (New Moon)

Appearance: Slim crescent (facing right side)

Approx. Rising Time: Mid-morning

Approx. Setting Time: Mid-evening

Phase: 1st Quarter

Appearance: Half full (facing right side)

Approx. Rising Time: Around noon

Approx. Setting Time: Around midnight

Phase: Waxing Gibbous

Appearance: 3/4 full (on the right side)

Approx. Rising Time: Mid-afternoon

Approx. Setting Time: Earliest hours of the morning

Phase: Full Moon

Appearance: Round and full, complete

Approx. Rising Time: Sunset

Approx. Setting Time: Sunrise

Phase: Waning Gibbous

Appearance: 3/4 full (on the left side)

Approx. Rising Time: Early evening

Approx. Setting Time: Mid-morning

Phase: 3rd Quarter

Appearance: Half full (on the left side)

Approx. Rising Time: Midnight

Approx. Setting Time: Noon

Phase: Waning Crescent

Appearance: Slim crescent (on the left side)

Approx. Rising Time: Earliest hours of the morning

Approx. Setting Time: Mid-afternoon

Now that you have a general idea of all of the moon phase, you can see how their timing might affect different spells. The next section will discuss spells and each moon phase and how to incorporate them elegantly into your spells and rituals.

Dark Moon Magic. Some people will call the smallest crescent waxing moon a "new moon" and the invisible moon a dark moon. You will have to determine your preference in your practice. This book will offer that the New Moon is the very first glimpse of waxing crescent moon.

This moon is a powerful banishment moon. It is not harmful to banish unwanted energies, but just be sure that you are in a mental state of "harm none" when working with this powerful moon energy. For those who practice harmful forms of magic, this moon would be the best for curses. However, that is against the Wiccan way of magic and will not be promoted here.

Consider the dark moon an apt time to banish that which is not wanted or is ready to leave but is still clinging on. Call it the "moon of serious banishment." Examples might include banishing addictions, negative entities or spirits, serious illnesses, and diseases. This moon has serious energy to help you clear and release the more difficult situations in life like cancer, a menacing stalker, and addiction to drugs and alcohol. If you want to banish your habit of drinking too much coffee or a needy ex who won't stop calling you for late-night talks, you might find a better opportunity on a waning crescent moon.

This is an excellent moon to look at your shadows, dig deeply, go beyond fear, and enter your cave of unwanted mysteries and miseries. This is a superb moon time to work with divination and powerful soul searching.

Waxing Crescent Moon Magic/New Moon. A waxing moon is a growing moon. It is going from non-visible to fattest fullness. A waxing moon has magnetic energies that help bring things out into the open. This is building magic, such as growing something in your life, setting up a foundation and adding the walls, developing and building a business, growing your self-esteem, and growing your financial success. It is a moon that can bring things to us through the magic of building and growing. Call it the "growing moon" or the "self-improvement moon."

According to some practices, a waxing moon can be considered the best time to work on matters that pertain to the self, involving new beginnings, plans, projects, and relationships. When you want to conjure or grow some new positive energies in your life, like patience, compassion, or a brighter attitude, then this is a perfect time. This is a moon of self-improvement, bigger psychic openings, artistic and creative endeavors, beauty, absorbing knowledge or new learning periods, and meditations to ignite more passion and inspiration in all of your work.

First Quarter Moon Magic. The half-moon in its waxing phase is the time of attraction. You might even choose to name this moon "the attraction moon" to help you remember its benefits and powerful magic. The previous moon, the self-improvement moon, was about going within and bringing things to the surface; the attraction moon is about pulling desired energies from outside of yourself to you. This moon is an excellent time for spells that involve things that you want to attract into your life. Typical examples are money, social and career success, and protection.

Love is probably the most popular choice, along with money and success.

This is a moon to attract people into your life, especially lovers and partners, but also friends, colleagues, clients, and even a pet or an animal companion.

If something has gone missing from your life, like a precious object or a wallet, you may cast a spell at this time to help you find what you are looking for. This is also an excellent opportunity to cast magic to find the house of your dreams if you are house hunting.

Waxing Gibbous Moon Magic. The waxing gibbous moon is getting closer to the full moon, and it is an energy-boosting moon to help you give some extra push to your goals and projects that need to make it over a finish line. It is the "boosting moon." It's all about reeling and going that final distance with what you have already set into motion and have been working on. When your work might be falling apart, stalling, stagnating, or is feeling flimsy, the waxing gibbous moon will help you push forward and through.

It is a good time for renewing strength, determination, and will power in all of your ventures and efforts and will help see you all the way through. Some examples of a situation where this is applicable are giving in to temptation on your diet, burning out from working hard on a major project for work, and starting to get distracted and lazy because you are tired and lackluster. Use the "boosting moon" for all of the spells to help you renew your efforts and keep going on.

Full Moon Magic. The most powerful moment of the lunar cycle, the full moon is the time when the Earth is between the moon and the Sun, and the rays of sunlight are bouncing off the moon's face and reflecting fully back to us. It is in total alignment. This moon is an all-purpose moon and has such powerful energies it can be used as a constructive or "building" moon or as a destructive and releasing or "letting go" moon.

This moon is for your most important and powerful spells. It has the most energy of all the moons and will give any of your rituals and spells the direct power and influence that it needs to manifest your intentions and goals. This is for the moments of significant change in your life that need the magic of the full moon to help those changes occur swiftly and smoothly.

You can plan any spell on the full moon, but consider this moon for your priority spells and incantations. What are the things that matter the most in your life, and how will you ask this moon for aid and support?

Any magic, meditations, purpose, or goals that are revolving around your openness to spirit, your psychic abilities, and development, dreams and divinations, and intuition are particularly enhanced at the time of the full moon.

Waning Gibbous Moon Magic. After the peak of the full moon, the waning begins. The waning energies of the moon are going to repel rather than attract energies, so this time will be the most important time to get rid of things, like shedding a skin.

The waning gibbous moon is a good time for minor releases and banishment spells, general cleansing rituals in your home and workspace, and even for your energies that you may be carrying over. You can cleanse personal objects, magical tools, and implements, your altar, and your car. This moon can be called the "Dusting Moon" as if you are just going around the place and dusting everything. Perhaps there is no significant buildup of unwanted energies, but it is good to do a maintenance check to keep things clear and open.

This can also be a good moon for closure with certain things, such as relationships that were not fulfilling for you or complicated business relationships that need to be let go of. This is a place for reflection and introspection. It is a nice time to take stock of how you are feeling about current matters in your life. Ask yourself some questions: what is affecting me the most in my life right now? How did my choices bring me to this place, and am I satisfied with those choices? What adjustments, if any, do I need to make moving forward?

Third Quarter Moon Magic. Call it the Waning Half Moon or the "Remover of Obstacles Moon." This moon can be beneficial with leaping over hurdles that present themselves on your path. Obstacles always appear at some point on our journey, and this moon can help you achieve an opening with your spell work to make sure that you don't stumble over the roadblock ahead. It is bursting away from anything that would set you off track or slow d your progress.

Many people will use a third-quarter moon to help deal with temptations. After all, temptations can be a massive obstacle in achieving your goals. Working with this moon during your spell work would help banish the roadblock of temptation, whether it is on your diet or exercise routine or involving study or promotion. Use the "Remover of Obstacles Moon" to help you stay on your path.

Another way to use this moon's energy for a spell is when faced with transition periods. Whether they are purposeful or something that you have no control over, working a spell to aid with transitions at this time will have an even more powerful impact on your path.

Waning Crescent Moon Magic. The waning crescent moon is helpful in cleansing and clearing negativity from all parts of your life. This is a stronger banishing time, as it gets closer to the strongest banishing moon again—Dark Moon. Whatever has been plaguing you that is annoying, concerning, or frustrating, (unless they are so serious that they need the Dark Moon), the "Banishing Moon" will help you.

This moon will clear the decks of anything that needs to get going. It has more potency than the previous moon for this kind of work, so if you find that you need even more power for letting go of something, the Waning Crescent moon is an excellent time to cut cords, tie off loose ends, and bring hopeless cases to a close. This is also applicable when what you want is more than just dusting off but not quite banishing something seriously from the dark moon. It is a swift and benign ending with a Banishing Moon.

Best Ways to Use Moon Phase Magic. So, what happens when your magical needs don't always correspond with the best moon timing? This has certainly been known to happen, and you may not want to be waiting for the ideal timing to get going on your practice of a specific spell. So, how do you work around all of that?

This is when you can get creative and think outside of the box. An example might be if you are trying to lose weight. You can use each moon phase differently to help you with your goals.

A Waxing Crescent moon will be ideal for helping you grow your will power and your energy to stick to your weight loss goals, while a Waxing gibbous moon will help you have those little triumphs over cravings of tempting foods. In a waning moon, you can cast magic to destroy or banish tempting foods that you know will be bad for your progress. You get the picture.

Always consider what you are trying to accomplish, and then consider what the current moon phase can do to help you with that accomplishment. You may need to get your goal outlined clearly ahead of time and look at the moon phase calendar ahead.

Your whole goal could be achieved in a deliberate casting that covers the entire lunar cycle. I guarantee that no matter what intention you are casting for, any of the moon phases will have strong, elemental power to contribute in some way. All you have to do is get creative with how you work through a moon phase.

Let's use love spells as an example. Your overall goal could be to bring a soulmate into your life. You can use a Waxing moon time to call your soulmate to you, and variations of that waxing moon can be utilized to help you grow love within yourself to draw them closer and to empower the love that you will feel when you come together.

You can also use the power of a Waning moon to help you let go of and banish any old cynicism or bitterness you may be feeling in your heart from older love partnerships. You can cast magic to release your wounds and heartaches and help you open more fully to love.

You don't have to use an entire lunar cycle to cast multiple spells for one goal. You can simply time a one-off, specific spell throughout the cycle and fit it in where it feels appropriate.

If you are eager to perform a spell, and it isn't the right moon time for it, consider how you can dynamically utilize the current moon power to help you achieve your goals. There is always a creative way around it.

Wiccans will also use planetary signs and signals, such as astrology, days of the week, and so forth, rather than just the moon's phase.

You may find that utilizing the astrology of whatever sign the moon is passing through to help you out. Days of the week all have specific energies and are ruled by different planets, and you can use this kind of energy as well if the moon isn't right when you need it to be in a cycle for your spells. Not everything will line up neatly and perfectly every time, and so it is up to you and your practice to find the timing that will work best for you and your casting.

Fortunately, magic is not an exact science; it's more like creative art, like fine cooking, and so it will take some playful experimentation and practice while you get acquainted with the moon and her powerful resources better.

Solar and Lunar Eclipses. Wicca will always have some kind of connection to the moons and the seasons, and a part of that ritual reality is there will often be a regular state of eclipse. You may think that this is too advanced, but eclipses are just enhanced moon/sun energies that need some special understanding to properly use them for your spells.

Eclipses are a unique moment, and you can enjoy feeling their power through your rituals and spellcasting for an even more powerful and beneficial moon and sun experience.

During an eclipse, time seems to stand still or hold on for a moment before continuing forward, business as usual. It has a charge of intensity that can be felt by everyone and when you can connect with one and coordinate your magical practices around it, you will surely feel the intensity of this power. It is like a time between worlds and will hold your spell closely and reflect it to you in a potentially magical way.

Just like the moon, the sun waxes and wanes; however, it will do this over an entire year, instead of a 29-day cycle, like the moon. The shortest day of the year and the longest night is the Winter Solstice, and the sun is only visible for a few hours.

This would be considered the fully waned moon. After this, the sun waxes as we move toward the Spring Equinox, and the days become longer and brighter with the Sun's energy. By spring, days and nights are equal in length. By the time of the Summer Solstice, the sun stays visible for the most extended period (like a full moon phase) before it starts to wane into the fall and by the Autumnal Equinox, where days and nights are equal again, edging to the darkest time of the Sun, the Winter Solstice.

So, with that knowledge, you can now look at the solar eclipse and how the solar energy of an entire year can be packed into just a few minutes of eclipse energy. Some have called a solar eclipse a "micro year" because of how the energy from a full year of the sun's waxing and waning can be felt in such a short moment.

The sun is whole and then partially or completely hidden by the shadow of the moon before becoming visible once again. In those moments when the sun is covered, the energy of a whole year's sun cycles is condensed, and it feels as if time has stopped.

The Moon's presence in this phenomenon is of vital importance as well. It is her shadow falling against the Earth's surface, appearing between the Earth and the Sun and bringing together and unifying the solar and lunar energies in one moment. It is a sense of wholeness and completion that occurs and can be so viscerally felt at this time more than others.

Solar eclipses can only occur in the daytime and on a new moon. This energy is a time for planting new seeds, ideas, and projects. Just consider how much more potent your magic will be with the full power of the sun backing up the full potential of a new moon! It Doesn't need to be visible to you for you to work your magic.

In many cases, a full solar eclipse is visible at certain times of the year to specific continents. All you need to do is know when they are coming to prepare accordingly. You can still harness that power without being on the continent where they will be most visible.

When working with the energies of a solar eclipse for your magical purposes, consider what kind of moon you are working with, as well as the season of the year you are in. Is the sun waxing or waning? What are the lunar influences? What time of year are you working with? Cater your spells directly to these influences, and watch your magic, spells, and rituals become empowered with this strength and energy!

A Lunar Eclipse. The moon has a monthly cycle, rather than a yearly one (approximately 29.530587 days). This is when the moon waxes and wanes and then starts all over again. The moon is completely dark and invisible just as it is becoming new again. A crescent moon then appears to begin the waxing journey, heading to fullness. After the fullest moon, it begins to wane back d into a crescent until it reaches total darkness.

With a solar eclipse, you feel the "micro year," and with a lunar eclipse, you feel a "micro month." During a lunar eclipse, the moon is full and then is partially or fully hidden before becoming visible again. In just a few, short minutes, the energy similar to an entire moon cycle can occur (only with a total lunar eclipse will this happen).

It is the Earth's shadow that falls across the moon, making us more aware of her presence and her relationship to the moon's energies. The Earth appears between the moon and the sun and the three of them in perfect alignment at this moment create a strong and potent lunar and earthly force. Both the Earth and the Moon are considered the feminine energy and so at this time, focusing on the Goddess is particularly helpful and beneficial, if it is part of your practice and desired in your work.

Lunar eclipses can only occur on the night of a full moon, so you will be working with that powerful full moon energy in your spells and rituals. This is a perfect time for letting things go, and you will be able to do that much more powerfully with this eclipse influence.

As with a solar eclipse, the lunar eclipse doesn't need to be visible for you to utilize the power of this time. You won't be able to enjoy every eclipse with your eyes unless you can be a regular world traveler! You can just schedule accordingly by looking for the timing of the eclipse to help you with your spells.

For your spellcasting work around a lunar eclipse, consider working on your psychic abilities and openness to spirit. It is a good time for working on clearing blocks and energies that are stuck. Reflect on how the moon's energy is full and what season you are working in. What kind of moon time is it during the year? What seeds were planted before it became full? How long have you been working toward something powerful, and have this moment to release it fully and give birth to it?

Consider all of the essences and energies of a lunar eclipse before you work with it. Check your moon phase calendar to find the specific dates and seasons for them and enjoy working with these extra powerful moments in time!

Moon Circle. All over the world, people gather to celebrate the moon. Whether they are Wiccan or Pagan, the moon has always been a draw for people to come together and celebrate. All over the world, they cast their magical circles and join hands to enter the space between worlds. Moon circles are always happening, most often at the full moon, and other circles convene at the time of the New Moon as well.

Most will always conjure magic at the full moon time, when the sun and moon are in complete opposition to each other, bringing us into closer balance with ourselves and each other. All over the world, on the night of a full moon, people are celebrating with candles, incense, food, and spell work. That is such a powerful energy to consider. If we are all working together on the same night for these moments, it makes the energy of all things much more powerful. It's no wonder the full moon has such a strong, long, and potent history.

A circle can be a couple of people or a large group in a room or sacred space, or they can be outdoors in the open under her powerful fullness and magic presence. However, as many people are involved in a circle, the energy is sparked between human life forces and the energies of everything all around. It will always feel more powerful on the full moon when you consider just how many people all over the world are sitting together with their fires, candles, tarot decks, and friendship, hailing the life force behind this luminous power.

Moon circles are a time for people to come together and reveal what has come to fruition. Whatever kind of circle you are in, if you have a moon circle, you will likely talk about what seeds you have planted back at the new moon, two weeks ago, and how that has come to fruition. The full moon circle is your collective harvest time.

Moon circles are great places to determine what worked and what didn't. It is the community where you can talk about your connection to her divine source and express what you have reaped from planting your intentions in the soil of your life. What was asked for? What came back to us? It is a time and a place of self-discovery as well as community discovery.

Moon circles are a place to dance and sing, sway and laugh, cry, and absolve our worries and fears. The moon lights the path for everyone involved to help you resolve any pressing matters with the love and connection of those who are there in balance with you. It is a place to release new intentions and manifestations into the world and to have others bear witness to our life progress.

You may not have access to a moon circle at this time, but they are not hard to find, and you can even join one online and be a part of a collective of people all over the globe who come together to share and celebrate. You can even start your moon circle and see who might want to join you and become a part of the journey of the moon's cycles.

It can be a fun practice to involve friends, family, or new acquaintances to help you and others explore the growth and expansion that comes from working with moon energy.

Bring your candles and your crystals. Bring some soothing tea and wine. Bring some honey oatcakes. Whatever the occasion calls for, a Moon Circle is a vibrant, bright, and illuminated time for you to get closer to others through the magical power of the moon.

Moon Magic and Healing Spells. With all of this new information about the moon phases and how to bring them into your spell work, check out these moon magic spells for your Book of Shadows, and have fun organizing your magic around the magic of the glorious moon.

New moon Spells. A New Moon Spell can be performed on the day of the moon or three days after. This is a time of new beginnings, opportunities, love, and health, as well as many other options.

This spell will help you form a bond and relationship with the moon's energy by inviting her back into her growth phase.

You will need the following items for this:

- Smudge stick
- White candle
- Black cloth

- Silver/white cloth (optional)
- Moonstones/crystals (optional)
- Blessing oil/essential oil
- Mirror (handheld)
- Pen
- 3 Sheets of paper
- Cauldron or fire safe dish

Decorate your altar with moon colors—silvers and whites. This can include cloth and fabrics, objects and candles, or crystals.

Smudge the area of your altar and where you will be working.

Cast your circle.

Wrap your white "moon" candle in the black cloth and place it on your altar.

Smudge the candle in the cloth and meditate on the darkness of the moon and her return to the light.

Try to locate the moon, either through a window or outside. When you can spot it, take your black cloth-wrapped candle and hold it up to the moon, and say the following:

Welcome back, moon who grows!

I am happy to see you again, and what you know.

Another cycle, passed and gone,

Now we are moving forward and along.

And we will find you growing strong.

And so it is!

Unwrap the candle from the cloth, and place it in a holder on your altar. Light it while you say the following:

Today is new, with the moon on her way,

With every tide, she grows bigger each day.

I am grateful for her return.

As I praise her, let this candle burn.

Face the east, where the sun rises, and hold the mirror up so that you can look over your shoulder to where the moon will be (again, you can perform this ritual outside, if you are in a windowless room). Say the following:

New Moon, bring me your guidance and wisdom.

Show me with protection, my vision.

You help me every step of the way,

I am thankful for your guidance every day.

With my thanks and blessings,

To you, New Moon.

So it is!

Place your mirror next to the candle on the altar.

Spend the next several minutes in reflection and gratitude for the growing moon. On the first sheet of paper, you can write d everything you are thankful for. Once you have written all of your expressions of gratitude, but the page on fire with your moon candle and let it burn in your cauldron.

On the next piece of paper, make notes about what you have NOT been doing right lately, such as mistakes, errors, poor judgment, choices with negative consequences, things that may have hurt you or others, and so on. Forgive yourself, and release these negative energies by burning the paper with the flame of the moon candle, placing it in the cauldron to burn out.

On the last sheet of paper, make a list of all the things you would like to have in your life—your goals, intentions, desires, and dreams. Be specific. Leave nothing out. Do not burn this list. Keep it until the next new moon.

Warm-up your blessing oil or essential oil over the flame for a few moments and then anoint your forehead, at your third eye, to open yourself to the blessing of the new moon. When you are ready, you may blow out the candle and close your circle to end the spell.

Full Moon Wishing Spell. This all-purpose, full moon wishing spell will help you capture the energy of the full moon for whatever your needs may be or to help you bring something unexpected into your life. You will need the following for this:

- A clear, glass jar (pint size or larger)
- Pure, clean water
- A bell
- Silver coin
- White/silver candle

You will want to cast this spell where you can have a clear view of the moon. That could be through a window near your altar or workspace or outside.

Wherever you are working, cast your circle.

Fill your jar with water, and light the candle near where your spell will be performed.

Sit under the moon, and absorb her light and energy for several minutes.

Drop the coin into the jar of water. Allow the water to settle until it has relaxed from the ripples of the coin drop and is smooth again. You want to have the reflection of the moon on the water's surface and shining d on the coin if possible.

Gaze at both the refection and the coin together and use your bell. Ring the bell three times while looking at the reflection.

Speak your wish or intention aloud (you can also ask the moon to bring you general good fortune as well).

Close your circle.

Bring your equipment back inside (if you are outside), and leave your coin in your water jar on your altar until the next full moon or until your wish has come true.

Waxing Moon Courage Spell. Add some courage to your plans with this waxing moon spell. You will need the following items for this:

- White candle
- Red candle
- 1 or 2 sprigs of holly or honeysuckle
- Oil burner
- Lavender essential oil
- Black pepper (freshly ground is preferred but not required)

Cast your circle

Burn the lavender essential oil in your oil burner.

As the fumes begin to enter the air, you can add the pepper grinds onto the burner.

Light the white candle on your altar. Stand or kneel if you want, and ask for courage for your specific goals and intentions, and whatever challenges lie ahead as you stare into the flame.

Use your creative visualization for several minutes to view your triumph. See the specifics of your success.

After you have spent time with this meditation, you can now light the red candle.

Stand in front of your altar, in front of your candles, and say:

> *Courage and strength, I shall possess,*
>
> *That all my fears become less and less.*
>
> *On winning ahead, on to the other side,*
>
> *On victory's road, I will ride, ride, ride!*
>
> *And so it is!*

If it is safe to do so, let your spell candles burn out, or you can blow them out.

Close your circle.

Waxing Moon Success Spell. You will need the following items for this:

- Yellow candle
- Something to carve the candle with (like a pin or sharp-pointed object)

Cast your circle.

Carve a symbol of success into your candle wax (money signs, rune symbols, anything that represents success to you).

Light your candle and focus on the flame.

Use your creative visualization to visualize your success beyond your wildest dreams. Get creative and specific. See yourself in a life of success.

Sit and watch the flame flicker and dance for as long as you need while you meditate.

Let your candle burn out and close your circle. Be sure to supervise your candle so that it stays safe.

Once the candle has burned out and the wax has cooled, keep your wax in a container or bag on your altar.

Banishing Spell for the Waning Moon. You will need the following items for this:

- Pen
- Paper
- Cauldron or fore safe bowl

Cast your circle.

On the paper, write d everything you want to banish from your life. Be clear and specific, and remember: harm none.

Once you have finished your list, read through it, and out loud if you want to make it very clear and obvious. Keep focused on your intention to banish these elements from your life.

Light the paper on fire, and drop it into your cauldron, allowing it to burn out. As it burns, see all of the things on your list leaving your life and being extinguished.

Now, imagine what your life will be like without all of those elements in your life (you may start planting those new seeds at the new moon and waxing crescent phase ahead).

Close your circle.

Take the ashes outside and bury them in the ground under the moon.

The Power of Acceptance Spell: Waning Moon. You will need the following items for this:

- White candle
- Paper
- Pen

Cast your circle.

Take some time to ground and center yourself and reflect for a little while on what you need acceptance with.

On the piece of paper, write d all of the things about yourself or life that you have difficulty accepting.

Then, write d all of the changes and challenges that you know you need to face to accept and come into terms with these things.

Light your candle and focus on the flame.

See yourself letting go of all of these traits, issues, or circumstances, and accept the new life you want to set into motion. Use your creative visualization skills to picture this happening. See doors opening for everything you want to go on, accepting them along the way.

See yourself in your third eye, feeling peace and fulfillment.

Watch the candle flame as long as you need to.

Let the candle continue to burn safely until it goes out. Close your circle.

Keep the cooled remains of the wax on your altar until the acceptance has proven itself to you.

Candle Magic Spells

Many have suggested that candle magic is one of the oldest forms of magic in our human culture and evolution. It may or may not be correct, but within the candle is the power and ancient resource of fire, which was how we evolved in specific ways and, over time, how we chose to worship in certain ways, too. Pagan religions of old not only used candles for their rituals and worship but also torches, bonfires, and flaming symbols in devotion to their deities. It was the only source of light at night until the advent of electricity, other than the moon, and so it is easy to notice why this sacred element was so honored and revered in magical ways.

Even after the invention of electricity and modern lighting, the fire continues to be a powerful force used in many religions and cultures for more than just heat, light, and a way to cook food. Candles are regularly used in various cultural traditions and practices and can be found in a majority of households for a variety of reasons. Consider the blowing out of the candles on a birthday cake and the lighting of candles at a holiday dinner with family.

Candles conjure a pleasant, warm, and magical atmosphere, and it is no wonder why they are still used in so many spells and magical rituals today. They are also the element of the South, and when you cast your circle, having at least one candle burning to represent this energy is ideal. It some of the most accessible and beautiful magic you can use, and this chapter will help you know more about what candle magic can look like.

How Magic Candles Works. Candles are a great source of magic for a beginner, as well as a seasoned practitioner, because of how they help you to focus and direct your magical intentions and purposes. It is a great way to assist you in strengthening your divination, visualization, and communication skills with yourself and with the divine spiritual energies called in to aid and guide you.

A candle is a beacon, announcing to the Universe that someone is calling for energies to unite and make new energy out of it. The power of all thoughts can be imbued into a candle's flame and magic, and that is what the basis of magic is—turning thoughts and energies into realities.

Magic is the act of sending a particular thought, goal, or intention into the spiritual plane to have it take shape and manifest in the physical world. Candles are messengers who help you achieve this magical goal. They are also channels or mediums to convey your messages or intentions and goals to those divine energies called upon to help you and guide you.

The candle burns through the wick, the wax, and the air all around and slowly disappears, carrying your message from the earth plane to the ethereal plane, striking a chord of energetic intention into the fibers and vibrations of the whole universe. To see your intention burning away through the magic of candles is truly a helpful way for you to put your purposes further out into the world. It is a symbol of the physical manifestation of your purpose into a message for the divine.

To go a step further, the candle is thought by some Wiccans to be the perfect balance of all four elements. The wick that passes through the center of the candle and leaves the bottom, like a root plunging into the soil, is the element of Earth. It is present to keep the candle burning, without which it could not burn all the way d to the bottom. The wax of the candle is seen as the water element. As it transforms from a solid form into a melted and watery form and then eventually evaporating as gas, it has all of the qualities of water's many shape-shifting forms, and it's what gets carried away to spirit.

Without oxygen around the candle, the flame could not burn. The element of Air, present all around you, is what calls the candle flame into being and keeps it burning. If you eliminate the air around it, with a candle snuffer or lid to a candle jar, you extinguish the light and the flame. And last, but most appropriately, the fire element is represented by the burning flame at the top of the candle, which rests close to the wax as it melts away and burns the wick as it continues to burn.

It is valuable to consider the magic of the whole candle and how it can establish the presence of all four elements, carrying your message away to the fifth (spirit). When you use candle magic, you are harnessing the power of the elements and how they contribute to every act of magic you are performing in your practice.

Color Magic in Candles. In addition to their elemental magical properties, candles come in a considerable variety of colors, and like with most things in this world, there is special magic behind every color that you use in your spells and rituals. Color magic helps us further direct our intentions and purposes by more clearly stating and representing what we choose to manifest.

Throughout the centuries and our history as a people, colors have carried specific meanings across cultures and have a universal identity and characteristic associated with each one. When you see the color red, you might instantly think of love, passion, desire, blood, and heat. When you see the color green, you might think of money, luck, four-leaf clover, and Mother Earth. Colors pull our energies in specific directions because of their symbolic associations.

Utilizing color magic with your candles helps to reinforce particular goals and intentions that are being set. You may see in your research that these candles will be referred to as "spell candles," but any colorful candle you find can be charged and consecrated for magical uses.

Magical Properties of Color. The list below will offer you some of the magical properties associated with each color. You may find other sources in your research that provide additional insight into various ways that color can have symbolism and meaning. Use your intuition when working within your practice, and let it guide you to the right color for your candle magic spells.

Red. Love, romance, passion, courage, intense emotion, willpower, strength, physical energy and vitality, health, root chakra, and fire

Orange. Power, energy, vitality, attraction, stimulation, adaptability (especially with sudden change), and sacral chakra

Yellow. Communication, confidence, study, divination, intellect, inspiration, knowledge, and solar plexus chakra

Green. Prosperity, wealth, growth, fertility, balance, health, luck, abundance, growth, renewal, heart chakra, Mother Earth, and Mother Moon of Triple Goddess

Blue. Healing, psychic ability, understanding, peace, wisdom, protection, patience, truth, understanding, harmony in the home, and throat chakra

Violet. Devotion, wisdom, spirituality, peace, enhancement of nurturing capability or quality, balancing sensitivities, divination, and third eye/brow chakra

White. Clarity, cleansing, spiritual growth, understanding, peace, innocence, illumination, establishing order, purity, cr chakra, and Maiden of the Triple Moon

Black. Force, stability, protection, transformation, enlightenment, dignity, banishing and releasing negative energies, Crone of the Triple Moon

Silver. Spiritual development, psychic ability, wisdom, intelligence, memory, meditation, warding off negative vibrations, psychic development, and divine feminine/female Goddess

Gold. Success, good fortune, ambition, self-realization, intuition, divination, inner-strength, health, finances, and divine masculine/male God

Brown. Balance, concentration, endurance, solidity, strength, grounding, concentration, material gain, companion animals, home, Earth, and balance

Grey. Contemplation, neutrality, stability, complex decisions, compromise, binding negative influences, complex decisions, and balance

Indigo. Clarity of purpose, spiritual healing, self-mastery, emotion, insight, fluidity, expressiveness, meditation, cr chakra

Pink. Partnerships, friendship, affection, companionship, spiritual healing, child magic, and spiritual awakening

Adding Herbs, Oils, and Symbols to Your Candle Magic. Color is vital, and sometimes you won't have colorful candles for every spell, and that's okay. There are other ways to enhance the magic of your candle spells with herbs, oils, and symbols.

Anointing your candle with sacred oil is a common practice and simply involves rubbing the scented and consecrated oil all over the wax of the candle before burning it.

This can be done on its, or you can add herbs to the process by rolling the oiled candle through a selection of dried herbs that will correlate with the magic of your spells.

These two simple acts enhance the power of your candle spell significantly and can help you open up even further to divine guidance and sacred manifestation.

As you learned in the chapters about the Book of Shadows, there are a variety of symbols, runes, and sigils that carry significant meaning and that can be used in all of your magical practices to empower your spells. With candle magic, you can carve the symbols directly into the wax to further carry your message to the spirit plane.

Your symbols should be specific to your goals and intentions, and you may need to do some research to decide carefully on which symbols are required for which spell. Trust your intuition, and let it guide you. You can carve the symbols before anointing them with oil and herbs, or after. You can also choose to use the symbols alone without any other ingredients. It is up to you, your spells, and your magical purposes.

Reading the Candle Flame: Divine Communication

There are many ways to read the magic of your spell through the flame of the candle. After the spell words and incantations are spoken and the candle has been lit, you can watch the flame to receive messages about the potential success of your manifestation. Some will view the results in the following way, but you may need to use your intuition in these matters, or research other sources:

High and Strong Flame = Manifestation is proceeding quickly.

Low and Weak Flame =T is not much spiritual energy invested in your intentions.

Wick with Black/Thick Smoke = Active opposition to your work (possibly coming from ill-meaning persons, or your unconscious mind is working against your intentions).

Dancing Flame = It has high energy for your spell but also very chaotic.

Flickering Flame = Spirits are present; prayers are being acknowledged.

Popping/Sputtering Flame = It signifies communication or interference with outside forces; something could be working against you; you may need to add more concentration and energy to your spell.

Goes Out Flame = A flame that just goes out indicates that your work is finished, and a stronger opposing force has ended the work.

Candle Won't Light = The spell cannot help you with the results you are seeking.

Candle Won't Go Out = You are not done working, and you need to spend more time with your spell.

There are many more interpretations to consider with candle magic that you can incorporate into your research and Book of Shadows, including reading the smoke and its colors and how the wax melts or drips or doesn't drip at all. Always tap into your intuition for guidance on these matters to help you align with your uses in your practice.

Once your candle has burned d, you can find fun in interpreting the melted wax, like reading tea leaves in a cup. The name for this technique is "ceromancy" and will require some practice on your part. It has a lot to do with seeing beyond the reality of what is in front of you and using your power of divination and clairvoyance. You can work on identifying shapes, patterns, symbols, images, and so forth, and try to determine what the "mood" of the candle spell might be or what is the final message from spirit.

Try not to overthink it, or you might skew and muddle the energy of your spells. Give some practice to it when you aren't doing important spell work, and have fun with it!

Practicing Safety with Candle Magic

Let's be straight and honest: fire is dangerous and can take d a whole house and the surrounding areas with one flame. It is significantly important that you practice fire safety whenever you are using candle magic or any kind of burning ritual in your spellcasting process.

Many candle spells ask that you leave the candle burning until it goes all the way out. If you are trying to conjure certain magic, this is a crucial part of your spell and needs to be considered. All you have to do is make sure that your candle is safe. Don't leave your house while it is burning, or check on it periodically while it burns.

You can also find certain kinds of containers, like flat-bottomed cylindrical vases made of glass, to put your candle in to burn. In this kind of container, the flame is contained, and even if it gets bumped or knocked over inside the glass, it will be safe.

Additionally, the oils can be flammable if not worked with properly, and the wax and flame can burn your skin, so take necessary precautions while developing your candle magic skills, and make sure you are practicing safe magic.

Red Candle Love Spell. You will need the following items for this:

- Red candle (try one first and then later if you want to work a more powerful spell; add more candles)
- Lighter or matches
- Rose essential oil

Cast your circle at dusk.

Anoint your candle with the rose oil. You can also carve a symbol into the wax that represents love or the kind of love you are calling into your life. (optional)

Light your candle and watch the flame for several minutes, or as long as it feels right. Meditate on the flame, and feel the love you desire growing inside of you. Allow that feeling to fill the space all around you.

After you have centered in this state for a while, say the following words, twelve times:

I ask the forces of Nature and Spirits all around,

I ask the Angles watching over me to hold me on the ground,

Help this love grow stronger and stronger within,

Bring this love to me from someone somewhere,

So that love I can truly win.

Let the candle burn out if it is safe, and close your circle. Try utilizing the power of a waxing moon to help achieve more powerful energy.

Healing Candle Magic Spell.

Disclaimer: Use healing spells, like this candle magic healing spell, in conjunction with conventional medicine, or medical treatment.

You will need the following items for this:

- Blue candle
- Green candle
- Sage bundle (smudge stick)
- Honey (preferably local)
- Salt
- Lander oil
- Springwater
- Mint

- Flower petals (white-colored)
- Bowl
- Piece of paper and pen

Use this spell for yourself, or for a person in need of healing magic.

Cast your circle.

First, carve a symbol of healing into the blue candle (healing color properties) and light it. Watch the flame for several minutes, meditating on healing energies and your intentions of healing.

On the piece of paper, write d all of the healing wishes and feelings you want to manifest (for yourself or someone else). Be specific. If it is for a particular medical condition, ailment, or sickness, describe what it is and what you want to happen in a healing way.

Next, carve a symbol on the green candle that represents you (or the other person). Hold the candle in your hand, and hold it out in front of you while you cast a mental image of the healing intention or the person's face or body. You may want to see yourself or the other person having already been healed. See in your mind's eye how they will look and feel after they are recovered.

Ask for the powerful divine energies to help you support this healing process.

Light your sage bundle and smudge your paper of healing intentions, the bowl, and the candle representing the person being healed. Let the smoke cleanse and purify these ingredients of your spell.

Put the paper in the bottom of the bowl.

Rub the honey on the top half of the green candle, representing the person, starting at the middle and working up to the top.

Rub lavender oil on the bottom half of the candle.

Set the candle on top of the paper in the bowl.

Put a ring of salt around the candle and sprinkle some mint and sage.

Add some spring water to the bowl and sprinkle the flower petals on top of the water.

Now, light the candle and see the person, or yourself, surrounded by healing, white light. Focus on the candle flame, and say the following words:

White light, candle bright,

healing love, healing light,

Let this energy suffice,

To help with healing overnight.

Bring all presence to healing and becoming whole,

Let this light bring full healing to the soul.

Let [me/person's name] recover fully,

From this challenge and difficulty.

Open up to healing grace,

From the divine, in every space.

I open up to all that is,

Healing light and love, give us this.

And so it is!

Allow the candles to burn out on there if it is safe to do so, and close the circle.

Once the candles have entirely burned out, bury the remaining ingredients in the soil outside.

Dream Job Candle Spell. You will need the following items for this:

- One candle, color of your choice
- Green candle (luck)
- Piece of paper
- Pen
- Cauldron or fire-safe dish

Face the direction of the south for this spell and incantation. Perform in the daylight hours, when the sun is highest in the sky.

Cast your circle, and face the south to perform the spell.

On the piece of paper, write out all of the details of your dream job. Be specific and include job title, salary, the city you will live in, benefits, and career goals.

Light the first candle, and say the following words:

With this candle burning bright,

I summon the dream job I will have by light.

Now, light the green candle, and say the following words:

With this candle burning bright,

I ask for luck to see me right.

My dream job waits for me to find,

All the luck I need to climb!

And so it is!

Now, take some time to meditate on your dream job. Take deep breaths, close your eyes, and see it in your mind's eye. Take several minutes to picture this in your head. Open your eyes, and focus on the candle flames for several minutes and continue to focus on that picture.

Now, read your paper aloud to yourself or quietly if preferred.

Light the corners of the paper on fire with both candle flames and drop it into your cauldron to burn and come to life!

Say the following words while you watch it burn:

Fire burning brightly now,

Cast my dream job into the light around.

Bring forward into my life,

With burning passion, brightest light.

So mote it be!

You can use this time as well to thank any deities for guidance along the path to help you succeed with your goals and purpose.

Allow both candles to fully burn out if it is safe to do so, and close your circle.

Keep any leftover candle wax to keep you focused on manifesting your dream job!

Triple Candle Love Spell. The power of three enhances and elevates any spell. Waxing moon phases are helpful for this spell.

You will need the following items for this:

- 3 red taper candles + holder/dish to hold all three together
- Red yarn, string, or ribbon
- Rose oil
- Yarrow oil
- Lavender oil

- A sharp tool to carve symbols into the wax

Cast your circle.

In each of the candles, inscribe a heart with a pentacle inside of it.

Now, anoint each candle with one of the oils so that each candle has a separate oil on it.

Bundle the candles together with yarn so that the symbols are all facing each other and touching.

Tie the string in a bow, and set them in a dish or holder that will keep them together.

Light all three of the candles as you say the following words, or something similar:

Life, Love, Heart,

I am ready for love to start.

I ask from above,

The gift that is love,

Oh, spirit, with all of my heart!

As below, so above!

And so it is!

Let them burn a third of the way d. Snuff them out and reserve them for the next night.

Repeat the ritual, burning d another third. Then, perform one last time on the third night until they go all the way out.

Watch for signs of a new romance.

Flame of Financial Gain. You will need the following items for this:

- Green candle
- Gold candle
- A sharp tool to inscribe in the wax
- Patchouli incense
- Pine incense
- Many acorns (smooth stones can be a replacement to represent earth and abundance of the Earth)
- Piece of paper
- Pen

Cast your circle.

Carve the rune symbol Fehu on each candle, toward the base.

Place them in candle holders and put the patchouli incense next to, or in front of, the gold candle and the pine incense next to the green candle or front of it.

Light the incense and get it smoking, and light the candles.

Draw another Fehu symbol on the paper, and put the acorns on top of it.

Leave the acorns (or stones) on top of the paper on your altar until extra abundance comes your way.

Let the candles burn d if it is safe to do so, and close your circle.

Burn Out the Negative. When you need to clear bad energy, low feelings, emotions, or anything negative around the house, use this spell. It's best used on a waning moon.

You will need the following items for this:

- Black candle
- Sandalwood oil
- Mint, basil, and white sage (dried)
- Bowl
- Baking sheet/parchment paper

Cast your circle.

Crush up your herbs together in a bowl so that they are in small flakes and pieces. You will be rolling your candle in these herbs.

Spread the herbs out evenly on the parchment-covered baking sheet (you can use your paper or a flat surface if you don't have the other items).

Rub sandalwood oil on your black candle.

Roll your oiled candle over the herbs, and cover it with the herb mixture. The oil should help it stick.

Set the candle in a holder and light it. It may spark a bit because of the oil, so take some precautions.

As you light the candle, say the following words, or something similar:

Negative energy, I banish you and send you far from me.

Bad attitude, poor spirit, lack of faith,

I say farewell to you on this day.

Divine wisdom, divine light,

Please bring me happiness and joy tonight.

I welcome peace of mind and an open heart.

Goodbye bad energy, I'll have a happier start.

Repeat the words three times and meditate on your energy is cleared. Spend time in front of the candle flame until you feel ready to close your circle and move forward.

Let the candle burn all the way d if it is safe to do so.

Crystal Magic Spells

Crystals are amazing conduits of energy and can be regularly used in any of your magic spells. Like a candle, crystals are excellent channels to add even more specific energy and magic to any of your incantations and magical purposes. As you have read throughout the book, there are several spells already that contain a crystal or gemstone that can bring you additional energy and success.

Crystals collect and receive energy and hold onto it. They will carry any information you wish to implant into them for a long period.

They can also collect energies that you don't want them to have, so it is common practice to cleanse and purify your crystals between spells or if they are used often for specific reasons.

Purification and cleansing can occur in a cast circle or at any other time that feels appropriate. Warm salt water, sunlight, and smoke from and smudge stick are all ways to cleanse your stones and crystals of unwanted, old, or stagnate energies.

Furthermore, once they are purified, you can then imbue them with whatever magical intentions you want them to collect and hold. Some Wiccans and Witches will refer to this step as "consecration."

All stones and crystals already have unique qualities and properties that will reflect certain energy into your spell. Some are more appropriate energies for healing and health, while others about psychic power and divination. There are stones for love and stones for protection and grounding. The list of possible crystals is long and will require additional research on your journey, so you can find all the stones that resonate most with your practice.

The next section will give you a list of some of the more commonly used and essential stones.

Common Crystals for Magic Spells

Agate: restores energy and healing, enhances creativity, enhances intellectual work, acts as grounding stone, works as protection spells for children, highly protective

Amber: promotes calming energy and impact in spells and for the person wearing or holding it, draws out negativity, releases physical pain, acts as good luck charms, brings positive energy.

Amethyst: aids with releasing addictions, calms and soothes ailments, relaxes and calms, enhances the psychic ability, helps control harmful behaviors, promotes psychic awareness, scrying

Bloodstone: abundance, fertility, physical health and healing, relief from grief or loss

Citrine: cleanses negative energy, provides focus and mental stimulation, aids work and employment, boost career, promotes honesty and communication, improves self-confidence and empowerment

Emerald: enhances creativity and imagination, magic spells for love, fertility, domestic affairs, prosperity, luck and fortune

Hematite: protection, grounding, a staple of the altar for its protective and grounding qualities, useful in a wide variety of spells, and balancing of the body, mind, spirit

Jade: dream interpretation, confidence, self-sufficiency, grounding, calm, serenity, peace of mind, body balancing

Jasper: red jasper for protection; yellow jasper to clear the mind and communication; brown jasper for concentration and grounding

Labradorite: dream recall, increases intuition, aids psychic development, helps resolve subconscious issues, associates with all chakras, provides wisdom and clarity, stimulates imagination, develops enthusiasm, heals personal addictions and dependencies, attracts success

Lapis Lazuli: openness, insight, truth, inner power, spiritual universal truth, interpretation of intuitive thought, psychic ability, soul guide magic

Malachite: emotional courage and support during times of spiritual growth, helpful during significant life changes

Moldavite: transformation, spiritual awakening, dream states, communication with the cosmos, spiritual protector, spiritual evolution, cleansing, communication with spirit guides, enhances psychic abilities

Moonstone: feminine energies, calmness, awareness, confidence, moon energies, soothing and relaxing, openness to ascension

Obsidian: grounding and protection, centering, healing, and clarity

Onyx: assists with making the right decisions, encourages happiness, good fortune, dispels negative energies

Quartz: many varieties:

- Clear quartz: clears the mind, amplifies the qualities of other crystals and gemstones close to it, logic, healing, creates a safe space for meditations, connection to the divine
- Rose Quartz: "mother stone," heart stone, love and happiness, protection for children and loved ones, opens imagination and creativity
- Blue Quartz: concentration and communication, the "student's stone"

Selenite: connection to spirit, a conduit between physical and spiritual realm, simultaneously cleanses and recharges, intuition, higher self, spirit guides, honesty, and purity, heightened personal vibration

Shungite: healing, protection, purification, psychic protection, grounding

Sodalite: Cooperation, communication, knowledge, intelligence, rational mind, education, and learning, wisdom, study, logic and intellect, inner calm, clears mental noise, self-awareness, self-improvement

Tiger's Eye: courage, willpower, loyalty, truth, luck, protection, truth-seeking, perception, cuts through illusions, brings to light manipulative or dishonest intentions.

Spend time getting acquainted with these stones and hundreds of others to bring into your regular spell work. They will enhance the energy of your magic, as well as the magic of your power and personal energy!

Communication in Relationship Spell. You will need the following for this:

- A piece of Lapis Lazuli (openness, insight, truth, inner power, universal spiritual truth, interpretation of intuitive thought)
- A part of Rose Quartz (heart stone, love, happiness)
- A piece of Sodalite (cooperation, communication, wisdom)
- A portion of blue cloth (sized to wear as an amulet or medicine bag)
- Cord (long enough to be a necklace)
- Small piece of paper and a pen
- One head of dried lavender
- Blue candle
- White candle

Cast your circle.

On the small piece of paper, write the following words: I am committed to clear and open communication. I am open to all sides of the conversation and can listen as well as I can speak. My loved ones have something to say as much as I do, and we can share as we talk to each other.

Light the white candle on your altar and state the following words: With this candle, I do light; bringing spirit, I do invite to help me open my voice of knowing, to speak with open heart and mind ongoing.

Light the blue candle and state the following: With this candle, I do swear to use my voice with love and care, for those, I am within sacred bond so that we may speak our true voice songs.

Set the blue square of cloth out between the candles.

Place the paper on the cloth between the candles on the altar, and lay your stones on top of the paper.

Place your hands over the stones and visualize yourself having clear, honest conversations with those you love. See the calmness and creativity between you. See yourself speaking your mind freely and lovingly. Charge the stones with the energy of clear communication. Spend as long as you need to in this visualization.

Place the piece of lavender on top of the stones, and gather the corners of the cloth together to make a bag or pouch.

Tie it with a long cord and then tie it around your neck so that it hangs over your heart.

Blow out the candles, and close your circle.

You can wear this medicine bag whenever you need a clear voice and communication within your partnerships.

Healing Crystal Spell. You will need the following for this:

- A piece of Shungite (healing, purification, grounding)

- A piece of bloodstone (physical health and healing, abundance)
- A part of amethyst (relaxing, calming, helps with harmful behaviors)
- Healing herbal tea to drink after

Cast your circle and sit in the center in a comfortable position.

Ask the divine to hold you close while you open to the healing wisdom of the universe (you may choose a particular deity to help you).

Hold the Shungite in your hand, and see a beam of light coming through your head from the cosmos, pouring into you from above and filling your whole body with loving, healing light.

See this light pouring from your hand into the Shungite, and ask for the divine to charge the stone with healing power and magic for you. You can create words to say to help you deliver the message.

Set the Shungite d, and repeat the following activity with the other two stones: bloodstone and amethyst.

Once all three stones have been charged with healing light, hold all three of them in your hand, and state the following:

These three stones, a powerful force,

Will keep me healed and on the right course.

Loving my wholeness, body, heart, and mind,

With these three stones, I will heal in time.

You can keep the stones in your pocket, or carry them in your purse. You can also make them into an amulet or sacred medicine bag to wear around your neck.

Close your circle, and brew a cup of healing tea. Hold your stones or wear them, and as you sip your tea, visualize your healing and how you will feel when you are healed again.

Dreams and Vision Spell. You will need the following for this:

- Purple candle
- A piece of Labradorite (dream recall, psychic development, subconscious mind)
- A piece of Moldavite (dream states, spiritual evolution, communication with spirit)
- A piece of Selenite (connection to spirit, intuition)

Cast your circle.

As you light the purple candle, communicate with your spirit guides, and ask them for what you want to discover in your dream state. Be honest and transparent, and let them know that you wish to receive a message and help with interpretation.

Place the stones in front of the candle on the altar, and speak the following:

Sacred stones of dreamer's sight,

Let my intuition open up tonight.

May you bring me powerful knowing,

And by this candle, receive its glowing.

Great Goddess, God, and Mother divine,

Let my dreams give me the answers and signs.

And so it is!

Allow the candle to burn all the way out on your altar. You can close your circle and go about your day.

When the candle is out, collect the crystals and put them under your pillow while you sleep. You may want to keep a dream journal or paper and pen by your bed so that you can write d any messages that come to you first thing in the morning.

Herbal Magic Spells

Herbal magic is a wonderful form of magic to practice, as it keeps Witches literally in touch with the powers of the Earth—not to mention the Sun, the rain, and the wind!

Most of the herbs can be found in the spice section of any grocery store. Only a few—elecampane, mugwort, hibiscus, and dandelion—might require a bit more searching, but they can definitely be found in natural food stores and cooperatives, as well as at metaphysical stores and online.

For people new to magic, a few practical tips are worth reiterating here. First, please note that the instructions for each spell assume that you have already charged your ingredients for the magical purpose you are working for.

Methods for charging tend to vary according to what it is you're working with, but if you're not sure how to proceed, you can use a standard method that works for almost anything: lay the herb or other object on an already-charged pentacle, and speak words of intention related to the spellwork you'll be doing.

Depending on your practice, you might invoke the Goddess and God, the Elements, or other spiritual energies you work with. If you haven't yet learned to charge ingredients, research and try a few different methods for charging various tools until you find what feels most appropriate for you.

Second, know that the amounts and proportions listed for each spell are general suggestions—there's no need to measure out *exact* teaspoons or tablespoons unless you find that doing so adds energy and focus to the spell. Otherwise, a rough estimation of the listed amount will do—as always, go with your gut instinct!

As for candles, which appear often in these pages, some spells include instructions for what to do with the candle when the spell is over, while others do not. If it's left unspecified, you can choose to leave the candle burning or snuff it out gently (with a candle snuffer or by waving your hand). You can use the candle again for atmospheric lighting, or repeats of the same spell, but avoid reusing candles for different spells altogether.

Finally, always remember that no matter the quality of your ingredients, how well you charge them, or how well you follow the spell instructions to the letter, your state of mind is the chief factor in any successful spell work. Approach a spell with doubt that it will work, and you've pretty much guaranteed that it won't!

Approach it with anxiety, and you're likely to get mixed results or no results at all. Some of the herbs used are;

Basil. As many Witches are well aware, basil is as versatile in magic as it is in the kitchen. This aromatic herb has long been used for medicinal and culinary purposes in places around the world.

A beautiful annual, with its waxy green leaves and purple or white flowers, basil makes a wonderful addition to your garden or window sill and a powerful herbal ally for your magic spells.

Chamomile. The tiny, daisy-like flowers of the chamomile plant have long been recognized for their magical, medicinal and cosmetic properties. Of course, Witches frequently use chamomile in the same way most other people do—to unwind with a cup of chamomile tea—but there are plenty of other uses for this delightful herb as well.

Cinnamon. Cinnamon is another herb commonly found in our kitchens that has a long history of both culinary and magical importance. Anyone familiar with its pungent taste and scent will probably not be surprised to learn that cinnamon is associated with the Sun and the Element of Fire, but it's also an Air herb, lending it more versatility than you might suspect.

Dandelion. Dandelion, from the French "dent de lion," or "tooth of the lion" is in our modern times considered a "weed," and many homeers despair every year as the bright yellow heads threaten to take over the lawn. But this ubiquitous herb has amazing magical, medicinal, and yes, even culinary powers.

Dandelion is a great illustration of the benefits of listening to your true voice and allowing yourself to become confident in your magical abilities. Magic at its best will cause you to see the world with magical eyes. So, the next time you see a dandelion patch in your yard or a field, let go of the notion of "pesky weeds" and embrace this mighty yet humble gift of Nature for what it is—an ally in pursuit of health, wisdom, and happiness.

Lavender. Native to the Mediterranean region, lavender has been utilized for medicinal, magical, and even domestic purposes across many cultures for thousands of years. For example, Roman soldiers used the wild-growing herb to wash their clothes and perfume their bathwater. This continued into the Middle Ages when washerwomen were called "lavenders". Magically, lavender is a masculine herb, associated with the planet Mercury and the element of Air. Witches often use lavender as an aspersing herb, dipping the plant in water and sprinkling it around the ritual space for purification before beginning a spell.

Mugwort. Mugwort considered magically feminine, mugwort is associated with both Venus and the Moon, although its Elemental association is Earth. Mugwort is considered a sacred herb of

Artemis, the Greek goddess of the Moon, which gives it its scientific name *artemisia vulgaris*. Many magical traditions associate mugwort with divination, and some Witches use an infusion of mugwort to ritually cleanse their ritual and divination tools. A powerful herb for dreaming, mugwort can be used to both bring about and balance out intense dreams. You will find a spell below to encourage lucid dreaming, as well as spells for repelling unwanted energies, enhancing divination, and protecting yourself during travel.

Nutmeg. One of the most pleasantly aromatic herbs used in magic, nutmeg is a seed, or kernel, of the fruit from the Myristica fragrans tree. The shell of the same seeds yields the herb mace. Nutmegs are evergreen trees, native to the rainforest of the "Spice Islands" of Indonesia. Since antiquity, nutmeg has been highly prized for its aromatic, aphrodisiac and medicinal uses.

Nutmeg has a long tradition of helping with a variety of medicinal needs, including being carried to ward off boils, neuralgia, rheumatism, and cold sores. Already in the past, nutmeg and its oil were being used in Chinese and Indian traditional medicines for many illnesses. Nutmeg encourages appetite and aids in digestion.

Rosemary. An evergreen shrub native to the Mediterranean, rosemary is a strong and fragrant member of the mint family. Magically, rosemary has many uses. It is still used primarily concerning its purifying properties—not only to repel negative energies but to actively attract positivity. In some traditions, it is thought to be able to summon elves and faeries. Associated with both the Sun and the Moon and the Element of Fire, rosemary is also used to encourage fidelity in relationships and dispel jealousy.

It enhances memory—both in terms of the brain and the heart— and one the most powerful uses for this herb is in workings for making oneself "unforgettable." Rosemary is also used for dreamwork and past-life recall, as well as retaining youthful vitality.

Sage. Magically, sage is associated with the Element of Air and the planet Jupiter. It is used primarily in magic related to clearing away unwanted energies from both people, objects, and places, gaining wisdom and healing from the loss of loved ones. The word "sage" is derived from the Latin *salveo*, meaning "to heal" or "to salve," which may point to an ancient understanding of the connection between this herb and the wounds of grief.

Sage is also a helpful ingredient in protections spells and workings for longevity, as well as clearing the mind and opening up the third eye. Some also use sage in spells for fertility and luck. In this chapter, you will learn how to use sage for cleansing your ritual tools, working through grief, and tapping into your inner wisdom.

Thyme. This tiny-leafed garden herb is another member of the mint family and has long been used to flavor soups, stews, and other savory dishes. Magically, thyme is aligned with the feminine energies, the Element of Water, and the planets Mercury and Venus. Said to be a popular dwelling space for faeries, the plant has long been used to summon and communicate with the faerie realm—wild, fresh-picked thyme is worn as a charm, or the essential oil is used to open the eyes to the faerie realm and receive psychic knowledge.

Basic Spells to Help You Practice

Spell of Abundance

You will need:

- Copper bowl (if you can't find one, you can supplement the solid copper for another metal, like a silver goblet or chalice)
- Three gold coins
- Fresh spring water (you can also collect water from nature- a river or a waterfall, or a natural spring if you know of one in your area)

Instructions:

Plan to use the power of the Full Moon for this spell; schedule accordingly.

Create sacred space at your altar, using only candle light at night to perform your spell. If possible, perform close to a window so that you can receive the full moon light coming in the window. You can also perform this ritual outside to get closer to the Full Moon energy.

Make sure your space is calm and that you are alone and undisturbed.

Fill the copper bowl half way with the spring water.

Cast a Circle.

Toss the gold coins in, one at a time.

Find the reflection of the moon in the water inside of the bowl.

Focus on the reflection and state the following words:

"I ask that abundance flow into my life.

I awaken my riches by Full Moon's light.

My intention is prosperity

And my gratitude will last from here to eternity."

Close your circle.

Leave the bowl overnight. You can leave it under the Full Moon if you desire, or keep it on your altar.

In the morning, take the coins and put them in your purse or wallet, careful not to spend them.

Law of Attraction Spell

What do you need to attract the most in your life? Love? Happiness? Wealth? Promotion at work? Psychic vision? Use this spell as a multi-purpose attraction for whatever your specific intention is. It is a spell to help you empower your energy to open to what you are truly wanting.

You will need:

- Two candles (color specific to intention)
- Paper and pen (you can use colored pens to enhance your intention)
- Cauldron
- Matches/ lighter

You can use your altar space or another area where you can focus and be undisturbed.

Make sure you are in the right mind space to work this spell. Any negative or doubtful feelings that you may have will hurt the energy of your spell.

Cast a Basic Circle.

Write your intentions on the paper. Be specific and clear.

Light your candles.

Read your intentions out loud if you like.

Catch the paper on fire with the flame of both candles.

Place the paper in your cauldron to safely burn.

While it burns, repeat the following words as many times as you can before the paper burns completely:

"Let me be seen, heard, and blessed on this day, harming no one on my way."

Close your circle before the next step.

Take your cauldron outside and feed the ashes to the wind if there is any to blow the ashes, or let them fall from the cauldron and waft into the air.

Instead of blowing out your candles, leave them burning or snuff them out.

Repeat this spell up to nine consecutive nights to help enhance the power.

If you aren't seeing any results, clear your energy and intentions, and try again after about a month.

Love Spells

When a love spell is performed correctly, the energy is fairly easy to control. Some people will turn to magick to find their true love, because they may feel lonely or desperate. Any type of love spell - whether it be Wiccan, Voodoo, Obeah, Black, Egyptian - can be cast. Using a love spell has many purposes, whether you want to enhance your love life, call upon a lover, actively seek partnership, or heal your current relationship, you can utilize a love spell.

Witchcraft Love Spell. This true love spell will help you recognize and realize that the love you have felt or not felt for so long has always been there.

Love is an energy that never dies in which casting this love spell will help you understand that you can gain the happiness that you desire and deserve. You first must prepare.

With this preparation, you must be aware that Witchcraft comes with a connection to all things. Use the power of your mind in perfect connection with natural and spiritual forces. Love spells tap into the power of thoughts, actions, and natural elements to bring your desired result.

What you will need:

- One piece of parchment paper
- Rose oil
- A wooden pencil without the eraser
- One pink candle
- Matches made from wood

Cast your Sacred Circle and begin by cleansing and consecrating the candle and anointing it with the rose oil. Once finished, light the candle. Put the parchment paper in front of you, then write your name on it. Draw a circle clockwise around your name, and then, besides that one, draw another circle. This symbolizes your soul-mate. Use the candle to drip wax onto the two circles while at the same time focus your desire on what your intent is behind this process and spell.

Build as much energy as you can for this spell. Once the circles are covered with wax from your candle, blow out the candle and say:

"So, transfer my will, my spell has been heard, as I will, so mote it be."

Once your ritual is done, you will have to take your parchment paper out to nature and dispose of it. If you choose to burn it, then you must hide the ashes in dirt or spread it in the lake.

If you opt-out of burning the paper, make sure you hide it well in the mid of pure nature. The candle is to be lit on the following full moon and you leave it burning until all of it is gone.

Herbal Love Charm Spell. This spell is a charm to help you release your blocks to love so you can attract it into your life better. A combination of herbs made into a sachet as a charm is a perfect way to enhance your openness to love. If you can't get all of the herbs on the list, that's okay! Just work with what you can find.

You will need:

- 5-8 whole cloves
- 1 tsp mugwort (dried)
- 1 tsp lemon balm (dried or fresh)
- 1 tsp St. John's wort (dried)
- 1/3 cup chamomile flowers (dried)
- 3 tbsps rose petals (dried or fresh)
- bowl
- 1 pink candle
- A square piece of cloth and string to tie into a sachet (like a potpourri bag)

Instructions:

Cast a Circle (basic or ritual)

Have your ingredients ready to work with on your altar.

Light your candle as you take deep breaths and consider your intentions.

Mix the chamomile, mugwort, lemon balm, and St. John's wort with your fingers in the bowl.

Pour onto the cloth.

Sprinkle in the rose petals and cloves.

Close the sachet with the string

Hold the love charm in your hands in front of the candle and see your whole body covered inside and out with white light. Imagine it pouring out of your heart and filling your whole being. It can even fill the whole circle you have cast.

Now let sweet, pink light come from your heart and pour into the white light, as you hold your charm.

Say the following phrase, or whatever feels right to you, three times:

> *"With this charm of loving herbs,*
>
> *My blocks to love I will disturb,*
>
> *To remove them from my life,*
>
> *Waking love and bringing light."*

Play around with the words to find the right meaning for yourself. The spell is about releasing unwanted blocks to let love flow through you freely and accept it openly.

Let the candle burn out of its accord (make sure it is in a safe space to burn at length).

Close your circle.

Wear your charm and keep it near you as often as you can. Sleep with it under your pillow even.

When the charm has fulfilled its magic purpose, you can bury it in the Earth, and/or, sprinkle the herbs somewhere, like in a flowing river to let your love continue to flow or grow.

Protection Spell

Protection spells are used to protect yourself from evil spirits and negativity, and you can also put these spells on other people as well. You can spell an object for protection, or even your home. Protection spells are best for when you need the extra boost of white light surrounding you. This specific Rune Magick spell offers protection from external and internal forces. This is the ultimate protection spell that will bring us harmony and give us that barrier from all aspects.

What you will need:

- Five white spell candles
- An instrument for carving symbols into the candle
- The incense that is either cinnamon, myrrh, or sage
- Salt
- Oil to soak your candles with. It can be an essential oil that makes you feel the most comfortable - a favorite scent perhaps.

Start by grabbing one of the five candles to represent yourself, carve in the rune "Algiz" and write your name beneath it. You can find this symbol online or anywhere you look. By now you should have made a Sacred Circle, so, place the other four candles on all the points - North, East, South, and West.

Next, place your representation candle in the center of all four and spread your salt in a circle around every candle, then pinch a small grain of salt directly in front of you. Clear your mind of all negative thoughts and light your incense.

Now carefully follow the next steps.

- Light the candle to the East and say: "Powers of Air, hear my call grant me your protection that is all I ask for."

- Light the candle to the South and say: "Powers of Fire, hear my call grant me your protection that is all I ask for."
- Light the candle to the West and say: "Powers of Water, hear my call grant me your protection that is all I ask for."
- Light your last candle to the North and say: "Powers of Earth, hear my call and grant me your protection that is all I ask for."
- Look directly up to the skies and say: "Powers of High, listen to my plea, May I always be protected by thee."
- Light your candle in front of you and say: "Banish my fears! I light with your light, I am guarded, well-protected and with a shield, I rise."

The next step is to stare directly into your flame and imagine a protective white light surrounding you. This light is warm and comforting. Breathe in your light and let the protection take over.

Healing Spell

The main purpose of healing spells is to rejuvenate your soul, body, mind, or perhaps your external life and well-being. It could be to heal someone else as well.

For this exercise, it is called the chakra healing spell. chakra is the center of energy in which there are seven different regions of energy in your body.

The Chakra healing spell is to balance out your emotions with your body to rid yourself of any negative energy and solely heal.

The only thing you need for this spell is one stone for each of the seven chakras, and six clear quartz stones before you can begin.

Lay on your back without crossing your legs. Place each stone to their desired chakras on your body. Place the six quartz stones like this:

- above your head
- beside each arm
- one in each hand, and one beside the feet

Come into a relaxed state, focusing on your breathing until you are completely at ease and calm. Do this for eight to ten minutes, and trust that the stones will do their jobs to heal and cleanse you.

Once the procedure is done, make sure to cleanse all your stones by running them underwater, or by placing them in direct sunlight to recharge.

Banishing Spell

The banishing spells work great for ridding your home or area of any unwanted presence. Usually banishing spells consist of protection and purifying your area. It's what most people would do before they move everything into a new home, or if they were moving. This specific elemental banishing spell should be done after you have cast your circle.

Go to the west side of your circle facing outwards and draw a banishing pentagram (pointing inward toward the earth) with your index finger, wand, or athame. The next step is to point your finger or athame in the direct middle of the imaginary pentagram, and move your finger outwards while pushing outward with your energy as well. Then say:

"Go, or be cast into the depths of the flood!" Move to the south and repeat your actions, saying: "Go, or be cast into the flames!" Move to the east and repeat your actions, saying: "Go, or be sent by the grinding earthquakes!"

Move to the north end of your circle and pause to collect yourself and close the circle. After closing the circle draw the final pentagram and say:

"Go, or be torn apart by the whirlwind!"

The ritual is not over yet, the next step is to cleanse and purify your home. Start by giving your house a thorough sweep with your straw brooms, vacuum, and dust rags. Make your house as clean as you can get it, unpack boxes if you have just moved, make your beds, do the laundry and dishes, etc... Once your entire house is clean and fresh, take some saltwater and sprinkle it everywhere, including inside cupboards, drawers, and closets.

When this is complete, light incense that is peaceful and relaxing such as vanilla, sage, or sandalwood, and walks around your whole house. Make sure every room is completely covered as you walk along every edge.

While you are doing this, ask for the blessings of your Gods and Goddesses to be in your house and for the house to be filled with joy and peace. Hang any charms that bring good luck and leave them hanging for a good amount of time.

Your spell is complete.

To Attract More Funds to Pay Your Bills

Ingredients

- A piece of paper which is a symbolic representation of money
- 1 pen with silver or gold ink
- 1 black ribbon
- 1 white candle, preferably scented

Process

Gather all your bills and dues around. Make a neat pile or regularly arrange them (so you don't destroy or tear anything).

Now take out your pen and write the following words on the paper:

"I am capable of having enough money to pay these bills and I will not fear these debts."

Once you have written that, place the paper on top of the pile and light up the candle to complete the spell.

Do not tear the piece of paper. Keep it aside until you have paid one of the debts. Then repeat the process with the remaining bills and dues.

Money Oil

Ingredients

- A small glass bottle that is not bigger than 7 cm
- 1 tiger's eye
- 4 ounces of almond or olive oil

Process

Put the bottle and gemstone under running water. If you have access to a stream, then you can make use of the power of nature. Otherwise, tap water will do.

Pour the oil into the bottle.

Then drop in your tiger's eye.

Close the bottle tightly.

Shake the bottle three times to fill the oil with energy.

Now you can simply open the bottle and dab a little of the oil wherever you like when you want some of that good fortune!

Spell to Attract Treasure

Ingredients

- 1 small mirror

- A small tin box (with the lid)
- Nine coins
- A small magnet

Process

Place the mirror d in front of you.

Lay d the coins one on top of the other (make sure you balance them right!)

Place the magnet inside the box (this symbolizes the act of attracting money.)

Chant the phrase below:

"Oh God or Goddess. Please attract treasure into my life."

Next, place the coins into the tin box and close the lid.

Keep this box in a drawer or closet.

NOTE: Treasure does not necessarily refer to money. It could be something intangible, like the appearance of a romantic partner, the emergence of new opportunities, or even a new experience.

Spell to Attract a Lover

Ingredients

- 1 small bell
- 1 rose-colored candle
- 1 piece of paper
- 1 pen
- A few drops of rose or jasmine oil

Process

Begin by writing d the characteristics of the person you would like to attract in your life on the piece of paper.

Once you are done, light up the candle and place the piece of paper close to it (make sure it cannot be burnt easily).

Add a few drops of oil on the bell.

Hover the bell above the paper and chant the phrase below three times. After each chant, you have to ring the bell once. Here is the chant:

"Oh God and Goddess. Allow your powers to attract the lover I seek into my life."

Once you speak the above phrase, ring the bell.

Repeat the process two more times.

Take the piece of paper and keep it with you.

Spell to Increase Sex Life

Ingredients

- 4 red candles
- Rose or jasmine oil
- Your favorite romantic music (preferably something slow. If you like, my recommendation would be Sexual Healing by Marvin Gaye. Always works like a charm, no pun intended.)

Process

The first thing that you should do is take a shower or a bath with sea salt.

Once done, anoint yourself with rose or jasmine oil.

Now it is time to set the mood, so play those tunes.

Once done, place each of the candles in the four cardinal directions and light them up.

Turn to each of the directions and say the following phrase:

"Spirit of (direction), grant the power of love and desire. So mote it be."

Make sure that you are doing it for each of the directions.

For example, if you are starting with the east direction, then you should face east and then say:

"Spirit of the east grant the power of love and desire. So mote it be."

In the same way, repeat the steps for each of the directions as you face it.

Spell to Attract Support

Ingredients

- 1 ceramic pot or bowl
- Potting soil
- 9 mushroom seeds, preferably ones with different flowers

Process

Fill up your pot of bowl with potting soil

Next, plant the seeds in the soil at different spots.

Once you are done planting the seeds, simply chant the below:

"As I plant these seeds

Plant support in my life

As the seeds grow

Lift me up from my strife."

Make sure you regularly water the plant and watch the mushrooms grow.

Spell to Find a Better Job

Ingredients

- Piece of paper
- 1 pen
- 4 white candles

A sage bundle

Process

Place the four candles in the four cardinal directions and then light them up.

Once that is done, write d the type of job you would like to attract. Make it realistic. You cannot say you would like to be the CEO of a company if you are just starting. You should ideally be writing d the details of a real job posting that you saw in the newspaper or online. Write d the job role, the company's name, job description, contact details, and any other information you can find.

Once you have done that, place the piece of paper in the center of the candle arrangement.

Face one direction and then chant the below:

"Oh, spirit of the (name of the direction), grant me this opportunity so that I may succeed in life. So mote it be."

Do this for all the directions.

Once done, return to your original position to end the ritual.

To Overcome and Enemy

Ingredients

- 1 pot of water
- 1 piece of paper
- 1 pen
- 1 tablespoon salt
- 1 tablespoon vinegar

Process

Bring the water in the pot to a boil.

While it is boiling, write d the name of the person you would like to overcome on the piece of paper.

Let the water start boiling and add the salt and vinegar into the boiling liquid.

Now toss in the piece of paper in it as well.

As the paper dissolves, imagine your fear of the person dissolving in the liquid as well.

As this is a simple version of a spell, you might have to repeat it a few times for the effect to take over.

Ending a Friendship

Ingredients

- 1 pot of water
- 1 black candle
- 1 piece of paper
- 1 pen
- 1 tablespoon salt
- 1 tablespoon vinegar

Process

This ritual is almost similar to the previous ritual because, in some ways, you are planning to overcome a bad friendship. It could be because your friend has been taking advantage of you or you have been in an emotionally abusive friendship.

Either way, you are going to overcome it. There are a few added steps because, in this spell, you are trying to overcome an entire relationship rather than one person.

Just like the previous relationship, bring the water in the pot to a boil.

As the water is boiling, light up the candle.

Take out a piece of paper and write d the names of your friend(s).

Now add the vinegar and salt into the pot. Once that is done, drop the paper into the pot.

As the water is boiling, chant the below verse:

I would like to free myself from this friendship for it is causing me much harm.

Once you have done that, wait for a while as the paper dissolves and then blow out the candle by saying:

"As I blow this candle, so do I blow away the powers of our friendship."

Black Magick Spell to Reverse a Curse

Ingredients

- 1 wok
- 6 white candles
- 6 black candles
- 3 cinnamon sticks
- A cup of water
- Stove or wood that burns easily

Process

This ritual must be performed if you are certain (or have the strong inclination) that there has been a curse placed against you. If the ritual is successful and there has indeed been a curse made against you, it will return to the caster. If there have not been any curses created, then this spell will not work.

With that in mind, let us get started on the ritual. Place the wok on a stove or you can burn some wood and place the wok on it. Remember that you should make sure that you are burning the wood in a safe place.

Do not cause a fire because of your actions, or else you are going to face worse things than a mere curse (like a burned d house for example!) I would recommend using a stove for now. You are just getting started. You can even get yourself a portable electric stove (just to avoid gas here) so that you make use of it in your room. Just be careful about those hot plates though.

Once you think that the wok is hot enough, begin filling it up with water until it reaches the brim.

Let the water boil.

In the meantime, place the black candles in a circle around the wok.

Light them up one by one.

Next, place the white candles near your window or on your windowsill if space permits. Light them up as well.

Now drop all the cinnamon sticks into the water and allow them to boil.

Once you have boiled the cinnamon, pour the liquid into a glass.

Take a sip out of the liquid and chant the below:

"Listen oh spirits of above

Listen to this holy hex

Turn around the magic dispensed

Turn around the holy curse."

Revenge Spell

Ingredients

- 1 piece of paper
- 1 black pen
- Rubber band
- 1 black candle

Process

This ritual must be performed only if you have been harmed in any way. This is a revenge spell and won't work if you are using it to cause harm to someone for the first time. One of the reasons is because you are going to imagine what the person did to you. If your imagination matches the events (it does not have to be precise, but it should explain what you experienced), then the spell works. If not, then the spell simply dissipates.

When you are ready to get started, write d the name of the person who offended you or caused you harm.

Now light up the candle.

Hold the paper in the light of the candle (but do not burn it).

Close your eyes and imagine that deed that was done to you. Try and add in as much detail as possible. You could even imagine how you felt at that moment. The things you went through and the thoughts that you faced. Then chant the below verse:

"This spell I shall cast upon you,

So that I may be protected from further harm that you do

So that in the future you will let me be

I will now have sealed this charm

And I will be safe from your harm."

Roll up the paper (it does not have to be a perfect roll). Tie it up with the rubber band and keep it somewhere in your drawer or closet (or any other place where no one can find it).

Once done, do not blow out the candle, simply let it burn away on its.

Boomerang Spell

Ingredients

- 1 black candle
- 1 tablespoon rosemary oil

- 1 piece of paper
- 1 black pen

Process

You begin this ritual by anointing the candle with rosemary oil. Simply dab your finger into the oil and rub it against the candle.

Now take out the piece of paper and write the following:

"Anything the against me shall be returned in full."

Light up the candle and then speak out the words that you have written in the piece of paper three times.

Once done, burn the paper in the candle flame.

Do not blow out the candle. Let it burn away on its.

Spell to Make Your Lover Forget You

Ingredients

- 1 piece of paper
- 1 teaspoon salt
- 1 teaspoon pepper
- 1 teaspoon cumin seed
- 1 pot of water

Process

This ritual won't work if the person you are trying to influence is your spouse. You can use this if you haven't committed yourself to this person already. Place the pot of water on a stove and bring it to a boil.

Now write d the name of the person on a piece of paper. Imagine the face of the person and then chant the below verse:

"From now on, I forget you

From now on, you forget me

For as long as I exist

I will not be someone you see."

Once you have spoken the verse, drop the paper into the pot, and then throw in the salt and pepper into it.

When you notice that the paper has dissolved enough, simply take the cumin seeds outside your home. Once you're outside, chant the verse two more times.

Throw the cumin seeds into the air. Make sure that the wind is not blowing towards you or you might find cumin seeds blowing into your face!

Spell to Cast a Hex on Your Enemy

Ingredients

- 2 tablespoons olive oil
- 2 tablespoons mugwort oil
- 2 tablespoons frankincense oil
- 1 black candle, preferably scented
- 1 picture of the person you would like to cast the hex on or an item that they had held or was in their person
- 1 pen or black marker

Process

This is a powerful ritual. One of the things that you cannot do is simply cast this on someone who does not deserve it. If you cast it on an innocent person, then there is a chance that you might have experienced misfortune in your life for a short while. So, be certain of your intentions. Make sure that the person you who are going to cast the spell on has wronged you.

How is this spell different form a revenge spell? In a revenge spell, the person who wronged you receives a punishment that has an equal degree of severity to the harm that they caused you. In the hex spell, you are going to cause an unknown degree of discomfort to the person (usually threefold as it follows the Witches' Karmic system that we had discussed earlier).

- Begin by lighting the black candle.
- Once that is done, pick up the photo of the person or the object that was used by the person. Write d their name on it.
- Sprinkle a drop or two of each the oils on the photo or the object.
- Pass the photo or the object over the flame, ensuring that it does not get burnt. If you have printed out a photo of the person, then pass it at a certain height above the candle.
- Once you have passed the object or photo over the flame, chant the following verse:

> *"As the heat from the flame*
> *Touches this object*
> *So does the heat of the hex*
> *Find its way to the subject."*

- Once you have said the chant, burn the photo or the object in the flame. If the object does not completely burn, make sure that you keep it in the flame for as long as it takes to repeat the above verse.

NOTE: While you are performing this spell, make sure that you do not have any negativity within you. Stop and meditate if you feel that you need to relax for a bit.

This is important because any sense of negativity might cause the spell to fail.

Intermediary Spells

In this section, we are going to look at a few practical spells that are slightly more complex and will help you improve your skills more. Remember that you need to make sure you are comfortable with the simple spells before you move on to this section.

Whenever you are ready, let us get started.

White Candle Spell for Blessing

Ingredients

- 1 white candle
- 1 tablespoon olive oil
- 1 saucer
- 1 photo of the person or 1 small piece of an item belonging (you can take a piece of their shirt or something smaller)

Process

You are going to be placing the photo or the personal items of the person under the candle. Some of the items can catch fire. For this reason, I have added the sauce as well. Simply place the object on the altar or the ritual space and the place the saucer upside d on it. Once done, you can place the candle on top of it.

Take out the oil and anoint the candle with it.

Once done, light up the candle

If you feel that you would like the person to receive something specific (such as finding true love or becoming successful in a job), then you can add that to the list as well. There does not have to be a specific way to do it, as long as your intentions are clear. For example, if you would like the person to get a job, then you simply add the line: "May you find a good job"

It is as simple as that.

Once you have completed the chant, you let the candle burn itself out.

You repeat this process for 6 more days. You should make certain that your chant is the same every day. Additionally, you cannot add new requests to the chant. Once you have decided what kind of blessings you would like the person to have, you have to stick to those blessings until the ritual is over. If you would the person to have more blessings, then you should prepare another ritual for him or her.

For example, let us say that you added a specific line at the end that focused on the person getting his or her favorite car. Then you should make sure that for the entire 7 days of the ritual, that is the only added line you have.

Candle Healing Spell

Ingredients

- 1 white candle
- 1 knife (preferably your Athame). If you do not have a knife, then you can take any pointed object (like scissors) as we will be carving into the candle.
- 1 tablespoon mint oil
- Photograph of the person you want to get better (or any item used by the person)

Process

Begin by taking your knife or pointed object and write d the name of the person into the candle.

Then anoint the candle with the oil.

Light the candle and sit d in front of it. You can either choose to sit cross-legged or on a chair.

Once seated, take out the photo of the person and hold it out in front of you.

Close your eyes and imagine the person the way they were when they were healthy. Imagine their laughter. Imagine them full of joy or think about what they would do if they were not ill. Would they play video games? Would they be reading a book? Would they be eating a nice dinner at a restaurant somewhere? Anything that makes the person feel "normal" again.

As you can imagine these scenes, say the phrase below out loud:

"Oh God and Goddess

I ask of you

Please help this person in his/her time of need.

Bring health back into their body

Bring life back into their soul

Bring joy back into their mind

So mote it be."

Now place the object or photograph in a safe place (such as a cabinet or a closet).

Let the candle burn on its.

Good Fortune in New Job Spell

Ingredients

- 1 green candle
- 1 black candle
- 1 incense of any type
- 2 tablespoons rosemary oil

Process

Anoint the green candle first. Once you have anointed it, light it up and sit d comfortably in front of it.

Make sure that your mind is clear of any thoughts. Should you like, you can always meditate before starting this ritual.

Light up the incense and allow the scent to permeate the room.

As you can smell the incense, close your eyes and imagine all the good thing that is going to happen to you with this job. Perhaps you are going to get a promotion or a raise. Maybe you are going to work hard and impress others in the office. Or you could even think about being an employee who is going to help out others when they need it. It is all up to you how you picture yourself as being successful in your new job. Once you have done that, open your eyes and chant the below:

"Oh God and Goddess

Thank you for this opportunity

So mote it be."

Once that is done, anoint the black candle. This is going to be used to drive away any bad fortune that you are likely to encounter in your new job.

Light up the black candle.

You do not have to imagine anything. Simply say the below verse:

"Oh God and Goddess

Please dispel any misfortune that might arise in this job

So mote it be."

Allow both the candles to burn themselves out.

Once you start your job, perform this ritual again after a week has passed in your employment.

Candle Spell for Getting Employment

Ingredients

- 1 green candle
- 1 red candle
- 1 bowl of milk
- 1 pointed object (preferably your Athame)
- Your resume or job application. If you have the resume in a digital format, then try and see if you can transfer it to your phone so you can use your mobile device instead.

Process

Take out your Athame or pointed object and carve the name of the company you are applying for into the green candle.

Then use the Athame or pointed object to carve the victory symbol (which is an arrow pointed up) along with your name just below the arrow.

Light both of the candles and place them on your altar or your ritual space.

Now, look at your job application. While still holding the application in your hands, close your eyes, and feel a sense of power flowing through you. Divert the power into the application. From there, imagine that the power is flowing to both the candles.

Maintain this position for at least 30 seconds.

Once you are done, blow out the candles.

Place the bowl of milk as an offering outside our door.

Courage and Wisdom Spell

Ingredients

- 1 red candle
- 1 purple candle
- 1 white candle
- 1 rope of any thickness

Process

This should ideally be performed on your altar, but it is alright if you are using a ritual space instead.

Being by lighting the candles and then placing the rope near them.

Now pick up the rope and start tying a knot. As you do so, chant the below verse:

"With this rope, I bind to your power,

To be mine for every hour.

To make me strong when I am weak.

To give me wisdom that I seek.

To give me courage as not to flee.

So mote it be."

Now, you can keep the rope in your person or tie it around your neck. When you head to bed, you can keep the rope under your pillow to find courage against your nightmares.

Spell to Calm a Broken Heart

Ingredients

- 1 strawberry tea
- 1 small wand or stick from a willow tree
- 1 tablespoon of sea salt
- 2 pink candles
- 1 small mirror
- 1 small bag or piece of cloth
- 1 one quartz crystal
- 1 coin (of any denomination)
- 1 bowl
- Jasmine oil (as much as you like). If you prefer, you can choose another oil for the purpose.
- A nice attire, preferably something you like

Process

This spell should be ideally performed on a Friday.

Before you are about to perform the ritual, make sure that you have taken a proper bath. Alternatively, you can even take a shower as well.

Once you have done showering, anoint yourself with jasmine oil (or any other oil that you have chosen).

Once you are ready, sip the strawberry tea.

Dress up in the attire of your choice.

Now light up the 2 pink candles. Once you are done, pick up the mirror and look at your reflection. Notice the fact that you are a unique and beautiful human being. You are perfect the way you are.

As you look at your reflection, speak the below words loud and clear:

"Oh God and Goddess

I stand before you

As I have heart broken.

But I would like to move on

I would like to be strong

Hear these words I have spoken."

Once you have chanted, take out the coin and place it in the bowl.

Repeat the chant.

Once you have completed the chant for the second time, take out the crystal and place it in the bowl.

Take out the bowl and place it near a window or outside your home as an offering.

For the next 7 days, you are going to do something that you makes you happy. It could be taking a walk outside or having your favorite lunch. It could even be something as simple as enjoying your favorite latte in the morning. Every day for 7 days, you are going to enjoy doing the things that make you happy. While doing them, recite the following verse out loud or in your mind:

"I am strong

I am beautiful

The past love won't define me

As my heart is bountiful."

At the end of those 7 days, take out the coin and crystal and bury them somewhere.

Home Protection Spell

Ingredients

- 9 white candles
- 1 small mirror
- 1 rosemary, sandalwood, or frankincense incense

Process

Place the small mirror in front of you.

Place the nine candles around the mirror in a circle.

Begin lighting each candle one by one.

Once you have lit all the candles, speak the following sentence three times, each time a little louder than the previous time you spoke the sentence. For example:

"The light of the moon protect my home."

A little louder: "The light of the moon protect my home."

A little louder: "The light of the moon protect my home."

Finally, light the incense. Carry it around your home and let the smell permeate to every area of the home. As you enter each room, repeat the above phrase once.

For example, when you enter the kitchen, say:

"The light of the moon protect my home."

Then allow the incense to spread throughout the room. Then when you move on to the next room, speak the phrase again:

The light of the moon protects my home.

And so on.

Once you are done, place the incense near the candles.

Blow out the candles in the same order that you lit them earlier.

Spell to Repair Broken Friendship

Ingredients

- 1 old scarf long enough to encircle a tree 18 times

Process

Hold the scarf in your hand and pass around a tree. Any tree will do for this ritual.

You should have a cloth that is long because you are going to be going around the tree nine times.

You should be going around the tree in a counter-clockwise direction.

Each time you go around the tree, repeat the below chant:

"Where there is pain,

Let the friendship grow again.

And once it has been done

Let it harm no one."

Once you have finished the above steps, you are now going to go clockwise. Make sure that you tie the cloth somewhere so that as you move clockwise, the cloth does not come off (as I said, you are going to need a long cloth. Or a very narrow tree).

As you move clockwise, speak out the below verse:

> *"May this bitter feeling end,*
>
> *And all ill intentions end.*
>
> *I ask that this be done*
>
> *And may harm come to no one."*

Finally, tie a knot when you are done. If you still have some cloth remaining, cut it off, and then discard it.

As you are tying the knot, make sure that you speak the below verse:

> *"This knot ends all bad feelings*
>
> *This knot creates new beginnings*
>
> *Once it is done, all hurt is in the past*
>
> *Let the friendship renew fast."*

Once you have performed the ritual, bring your hands together, and thank the tree for helping you. As you are heading back home, try and think of the many ways that you can reconcile with your friend. Choose one option and go ahead and do it. Make sure that your sentiments are genuine and that you care about the friendship.

Spell to Repair a Broken Relationship

Ingredients

- 2 silver pins
- 1 red candle
- 1 red ruby, or any other red crystal
- A couple of red roses, or any other red flowers
- 1 red cloth

Process

Spread out the cloth on your altar or your ritual space.

Place the candle in the middle of the cloth.

Now place one red rose to the right of the candle and one red rose to the left of the candle.

Place the gemstone in front of your candle.

Once you have completed the above arrangements take the two pins and pierce the candle. Place one pin on the top area of the candle and the other on the bottom area of the candle.

Now light the candle and let it burn until it reaches the first pin. When it does, speak out the below words loud and clear:

"As this pin departs the candle

So too does the differences in our relationship

Bring is back together

As we face future trials and hardship."

Continue repeating this chant until the flames reach the second pin. Once they do, you are going to use the name of your lover or partner.

"Bring (you lover's name) and me back together

Let us start our lives anew

Fill our lives with joy and laughter

Let the separations be few."

Once you have done the ritual, it is time to do the hard part. This might not be easy because sometimes it might not have been your fault that the relationship has reached the point that it has now. But go ahead and reach out to the person. Talk to them and explain that you would like them to get back together again. See if you both can reach some sort of compromise.

Spell for Nervous Travelers

Ingredients

- 1 stone (you can get any stone that you want, even from your backyard)
- 1 yellow candle
- 1 Lavender essential oil
- Yellow paint
- Violet paint
- 1 paintbrush

Process

Light up the candle and hold the stone in your hands.

Now stand up, face east, and then paint the stone yellow.

As you notice the paint drying, imagine yourself arriving safely at your destination. If you do not have a clear idea of how your destination looks like (for example, you might be visiting a country for the first time), then simply look up pictures of it online or in a magazine. Imagine exploring those beautiful vistas when you arrive at your destination.

Now pick up the second stone and continue to face east.

Paint the second stone purple. Bring their stone to eye level and then chant the below:

"I call upon the spirit of the east,

Fill this stone with your blessing and protection.

I pray for a safe journey from (departing location)

to (arriving location)

Protect me and let me reach safely to my destination."

Now hold both the yellow and purple stone in one hand (you don't have to bring them to eye level) and then repeat the above verse 7 more times.

Once you have completed the ritual, keep the stones with you until the moment you are departing for your journey.

Spell to Help You in Your Business

Ingredients

- 1 bunch of basil
- 1 bowl of water
- 1 crystal of your choice
- 2 or 3 grains of rice

- 1 bunch of mint leaves

Process

Before you even get started on this ritual, make sure that you stir the basil and mint leaves in the water for at least an hour. Now and then, simply stir the basil around (it does not matter if you stir it clockwise or counter-clockwise).

Now you are going to bless your office or workplace, but you are not going to be there. For this, pick up the bowl in your hands and then start walking in a circle.

Start in the east, sprinkle some water, and then begin moving in a circle. You need to say the below verse three times:

"Let my business prosper

Let the business grow

Let there be a success

Let the good fortunes flow."

You should return to your original position (the east direction). Make sure that you have spoken the verse three times before reaching the east position.

After you reach the original position, put the bowl and say:

"So mote it be."

Now add the crystal into the bowl. Allow it to sit there for at least 10 minutes.

Next, add in the grains of rice and let that sit in there for 10 minutes as well.

Finally, remove the crystal and keep the bowl outside your home as an offering.

Take the crystal with you and place it in the drawer where you keep your checkbook. Alternatively, you can keep it near your accounts book or the computer you use to place your orders.

If you have a warehouse, then you can keep this crystal anywhere in your warehouse office.

Spell to Promote Peace

Ingredients

- 2 white candles
- 1 piece of jewelry of any kind
- 2 white lilies or white flowers of any kind
- 1 clear quartz crystal
- 1 large shell
- 1 coin of any denomination
- 1 picture or drawing of a dove (you can draw the dove on any piece of paper using any pen)
- 1 sprig of olive
- 1 chamomile tea

Process

Place the white candles on your altar or in your ritual space.

Light both of them up.

Now hold the crystal in your hands and close your eyes. Imagine what the world looks like it was filled with peace. This imagery does not have to do anything with a specific idea of peace. Rather, what do you feel peace should look like. It could be thought of as people helping the poor. It could also be images of the pride parade that

272

you had attended recently. It could be images of people sharing food.

Remember, these images do not have to be something on a grand scale. Rather, it should reveal the good side of humanity. You can even use the news as inspiration. Was there a piece of news about someone rescuing people from the fire? Was there a local story about cops banding together to help the community? Anything that shows the good nature of humanity can be used here.

Take about 5 minutes to imagine humanity's best side.

Now place the picture or drawing of the dove near the candle and then say the words below:

"Fly into the air and dove that carries peace

Remove the hatred and spread the love

Fill the minds of everyone with thoughts of love

As you look d on us from high up above."

Place the coin into the shell and repeat the above verse.

Now place the sprig of olive on the picture or photo of the dove.

Go ahead and heat some chamomile tea. Drink it and feel the tea calming you. This is the peace that you would like the world to feel.

As you drink the tea, repeat the below verse three times:

"Fly into the air and dove that carries peace

Remove the hatred and spread the love

Fill the minds of everyone with thoughts of love

As you look d on us from high up above."

Spell When a Pet Dies

Ingredients

- 3 small white candles
- 1 rosemary essential oil
- Something that reminds you of your pet — a lead perhaps, or a collar
- A nice attire, preferably something you like wearing. Try not to make the clothing too casual. Keep it either formal or semi-formal.

Process

The first thing that you are going to do is take a nice bath or shower.

Once you have finished your bath, anoint yourself with the rosemary oil.

Dress up in your attire.

Use the rosemary oil to anoint the candles as well.

Now light them up and sit d in front of them.

Hold the item of your pet in front of you. Now close your eyes and imagine all the fond memories that you had with your pet. If you ever feel like you are about to cry, then let the tears flow.

Remember, your tears are simply a symbol of the love you have for your pet. There is nothing to be ashamed of when you are shedding tears for the lives that were close to us.

Sit d for about 5 minutes or so in respectful silence with fond memories of you and your pet as a company. If you would like to sit d for a longer period, you can do that as well.

Once you are ready, open your eyes and say the below verse slowly, but clearly:

"Be at peace

Thank you for the joy you brought in my life

I shall cherish our memories forever."

NOTE: Grief is not easy to handle. But know that by performing this ritual, you are only saying goodbye to the grief that you feel inside so that you can create space for the love and happiness you felt when your pet was alive.

These positive feelings are what you are going to live with.

These positive feelings are how you are going to cherish the memories of your pet. For those using this ritual, I may personally not be a big contribution, but I would still like to say, may your pet rest in peace.

Luck Spell

Lucky Object Spell. Here are some important reminders for a Wiccan Luck Spell:

Harm None or your spell will not work;

In addition to casting a spell or charming your talisman, you still have to put in the effort to achieve your dreams and goals while you carry it with you. A talisman, charm, or spell will help you open to the right moment for luck, but you have to do the work to be ready and open to it.

You will need the following for this:

- A unique object, like a crystal, gemstone, piece of jewelry, amulet, or another item
- Three gold coins

Cast a circle as you usually would.

On the floor, your altar space, or your work table, arrange the coins in a triangle around your talisman or object.

Touch each coin, one by one, and touch each coin with your dominant index finger. As you touch the coin, speak the following three times:

I ask the Earth, the Moon,

and the Sun to imbue luck into my talisman.

With grateful thanks and gratitude,

I look for luck that is ever true.

And so it is!

Visualize light around your talisman as you ask for it to enhance with the powers of luck.

Modification: You can add candles to your spell to enhance the power and arrange them in a triangle with the coins so that your talisman is surrounded by candlelight and coin magic energy.

Meditate on the feelings of luck and receiving gifts of luck from the universe.

Close your circle, and keep your talisman on your person at all times. Do not reveal its purpose to anyone.

Bye, Bye Bad Luck Spell. Some say all your troubles come at once, and when they do, you can feel it. This spell is here to help remove the energies that cause a string of bad luck or challenging incidences.

You will need the following items for this:

- Parchment paper
- Black pen
- Long, thin green candle (luck and prosperity)
- Matches
- Fireproof bowl or cauldron

Thoroughly clean your house to purge any unwanted energies. You may want to smudge every room as well.

Cast a circle where you want to work.

On a blank paper, write d all of the adverse incidences in detail in order of how they happened. Summarize how it made you feel and why it feels like a "bad luck" streak.

Light the candle, and set fire to the paper when you are ready (you may want to read it out loud to announce the energy you are trying to clear).

Drop the paper into the bowl or cauldron and let it burn.

While the paper burns say the following in any variation: Bad luck moments and misfortunes of the recent past, I burn and release you now; you cannot last.

Let the paper burn away and scatter the ashes outside of your house, perhaps on the street to get them far away from you.

Close your circle and feel some newfound positive energy!

Basic Wiccan Good Luck Spell. The power of this spell is enhanced when performed on a waxing or full moon and is best used to strengthen and empower an already existing goal or intention of success.

You will need the following for this:

- Frankincense incense
- Orange or gold candles, 3 pcs
- Pen and paper

Cast your circle.

Arrange the candles on your altar or preferred workspace in a triangle. Do not light them yet.

Speak the following words: Goddess, God, Spirits, and Guides, thank you for your assistance and light. I ask you now for help with my goal, to [insert your goal or intention here]. I am looking for luck while I work to achieve, which will bring me the success that I need. And so it is!

Visualize how your life would look if you had already accomplished your goals and had success. Feel how it would feel to be in this life, with that joy and prosperity.

Meditate for a while in this state and let yourself fall deeper and deeper into this meditation. Clear your mind and let yourself open to guidance from spirit.

When you go into your intuition, you will receive a message from the spirit—a symbol, a word, or an idea. Write it d on a piece of paper, whatever comes up.

Take the piece of paper with the image or words, and place it in the center of the triangle made of candles.

As you light each candle, state the following: Sacred fire, sacred light, ignite my highest good tonight.

Sit with the burning candles and the image you drew, and meditate on the luck you already have had and more coming your way, opening your heart to even more good fortune and success.

Express gratitude to your deities or spirit guides, and close your circle.

Bury your paper in the ground outside, and say the following: Sacred earth, sacred light, seal my dream with highest good tonight.

Your luck will arrive in a way that is exactly right for you. Be open to it and trust the energies that come for you.

Good Luck!

Pass the test Luck Spell. This spell gives you good luck on exams and tests. You still have to study, but this spell will give you a boost of power and energy to help you succeed on the big day.

You will need the following items for this:

- Green candle
- An object to symbolize what the exam is testing you on (math, science, a notebook from your class, a textbook, a pop quiz, etc.)
- Lavender, Chamomile, and Rosemary, fresh or dried

The night before your exam is the best time to perform this spell magic.

You can cast the spell in a circle at your altar or wherever you want your workspace to be.

Light the candle with focus and intention about passing the test.

Scatter the herbs over your symbolic object (you can cover the object with parchment or muslin cloth if you are worried about herbs being on it)

Spread the herbs around with your hand. Breathe in the aromas. Visualize seeing the grade you want on your test.

Chant the following three times: Good fortune, hard work, and luck be by my side; I will pass my test with pride.

Blow out your candle, and get a good night's sleep!

Good Luck!

Conclusion

Spells are tools of manifestation. They are an act of powerful, creative, and energetic force and are managed and delivered to the Universe of possibilities by your very hands.

To work with a spell and cast it into the energy of all things is to work with the divine power of all life. A spell is a tool of connection to your practice, to yourself, to the God and Goddess, or whatever life-force energies you may worship and devote your energy to.

Whether you are Wiccan, Witch, Pagan, or otherwise, this book is a simple and effective tool to help you discover your power and path toward working more deeply with the magic of spell work in your practice.

This journey has everything to do with practicing safe and effective magic and will give you all of the guidance you need to take your trip to the next level. If you have been working with Wicca for a while now, you may be looking for some fresh spell ideas to add to your Book of Shadows.

For the beginner, this is a great companion to start your spells and finding the ones that will help you explore and manifest possibilities in your everyday life.

Other Books by Dora McGregor

Check all!! Visit the following link:

www.wiccantribe.com

Wicca for Beginners

Wiccan Traditions and Beliefs, Witchcraft Philosophy, Practical Magic, Candle, Crystals and Herbal Rituals

Wicca Moon Magic

A Wicca Grimoire on Moon Magic Power with Moon Spells and Rituals for Witchcraft Practitioners and Beginners

Wiccan Spells

A Book of Shadows for Wiccans, Witches, and Practitioners with Candle, Crystal, Herbal, Healing, Protection Spells for Beginners

Wicca Starter Kit

2 Manuscripts: Wicca for Beginner, Wiccan Spells

Dora McGregor

© Copyright 2019 Dora McGregor

All rights reserved

www.wiccantribe.com

CPSIA information can be obtained
at www.ICGtesting.com
Printed in the USA
LVHW041146151120
671606LV00005B/121

9 781801 141024